FOCUS, REFOCUS AND MAINTAINING FOCUS

Illustrating the Life and Ministry of Nehemiah, a Focused, Fearless and Faithful Follower of the Heavenly Father

Bishop L. E. Freeman

ISBN NUMBERS

Paperback 979-8-9872445-0-0

eBook 979-8-9872445-1-7

By Bishop Lonnie Freeman, Founder and Pastor of

Emmanuel Christian Center Church

Dedication

This volume is lovingly dedicated to my Kentucky wife of forty-four years and counting, Pamela Whitlow Freeman, my daughter Lori Freeman Jamar and her husband Darrius, my sons Jeremy and Aaron Freeman both are musicians at Emmanuel Christian Center Church, and both are teachers in the Public School system. My family has supported me in the writing of this book.

I also want to dedicate this volume to my dad, Lonnie Ellis Freeman, my mom, Ardelia Nash Freeman, my brothers Walter, Dennis and Pastor William Freeman, my sister Vera Martin Moore and my grandmothers, Eunice Davis Freeman and Blanch Moon Nash. In God's greater wisdom, these loved ones have departed into the presence of the Lord, may they all rest in peace.

To the past and present members of Emmanuel Christian Center Church in Leighton, Alabama where these lessons from the book of Nehemiah were delivered for the first time, thank you so much for being a great audience and a laboratory in which these lessons from Nehemiah were generalized. Much more meaningful blessings to those whose lives were blessed by the initial hearing of these lessons and to those whose lives will be blessed by the reading and applying the principles found in this volume.

TABLE OF CONTENT

HOW TO USE THIS BOOK

This book was written to help the lay population in the Body of Christ to understand this powerful and interesting book of Nehemiah. Because of this perspective, the book was written from a layman's point of view and not from a scholarly perspective. What you are about to read is by no means a thorough or exhaustive work on the book of Nehemiah. I share this volume with you as a fellow learner in a classroom trying to learn from this fearless and faithful layman and this favored and focused leader who has a deep care and concern for God and for God's people. I tried to read each one of the chapters of the book in a way that when a thought is found, that thought would be the essence for that chapter's lesson. This method was continued throughout the thirteen chapters. Nearly every verse in the thirteen chapters is accounted for in this presentation.

I believe the book will appeal to the individual as well as for those in a Bible study group using the thirteen chapters. The presentation was first delivered in the form of weekly sermons. After deciding to use the material for a book, I rearranged and added additional information so the work can be used as a "type" of commentary as well. The preacher may use the chapters for sermons; adding or deleting as needed. The individual may read the lessons presented for their personal spiritual enrichment and edification. My hope is that the words on the following pages will be a blessing to you as it was to me in preparing it for you!

INTRODUCTION

Somewhere on the pendulum from Focus, to Refocus, and then Maintaining Focus, you and I can be found. Among us are those who have never focused or concentrated on Jesus and his mission. Why? Is it because their priorities have always been on themselves or some other interest thus hindering them from focusing on God and what He wants out of their lives? Then there are those who once were committed, they knew what God wanted and sought to do his will by concentrating on him. But now, this person has allowed something or someone to hinder or blur their vision and now need to Refocus.

Yet still, there are those who have eagle vision, praying and watching and they are sensitive to the voice of God through the Holy Ghost and God's word. These Christians are moving in their purpose and the destiny God has ordained for them. They are endeavoring to bring in His fullness, His kingdom, and His will on earth. They like Isaiah who have seen the Lord high and lifted up and are Maintaining their focus. These Christians don't blame the distractions that they face which could cause them to get out of alignment, they just improve their focus.

My mission and purpose is to challenge the Body of Christ to focus, refocus as needed and then maintain their focus and attention on the Lord Jesus Christ. Each one of us as children of the Most High need to get sold out to God, get fanatic for Jesus, and go crazy for Him! I encourage the body of Christ to go after Him with all you got. We must learn to focus in the midst of opposition. We are living in a darkened age, a generation of evildoers as the Bible describes them. We are living in a society that is saturated with sensuality, social status and sexuality competing for man's soul.

We are living in an untoward and perverse generation, a nation where evil is called good and good is called evil. We live in an age where people get mad and ostracize you, persecute and reject you for telling them what is right based on the scriptures! They will argue with you over morals that Jesus has already established.

In spite of the opposition, we must persevere and live out the purpose for which Jesus has apprehended us for. Paul tells us in Philippians 3:12-14, "Not as though I had already attained, either were already perfect; but I follow after, if that I may apprehend that for which also I am apprehended of Christ Jesus-Brethren, I count not myself to have apprehended; but this one thing I do, forgetting those things which are behind, and reaching forth unto those things which are before, I press toward the mark for the prize of the high calling of God in Christ Jesus."

Christians are harboring bitterness, hatred, pride and lewdness in their heart with no intentions of repenting yet wanting to be involved in ministry. This kind of behavior is in opposition to the lifestyle God wants to use in His ministry and for His glory. God still does not give us an EXCUSE for not seeking Him with our whole heart and focusing on what He wants out of our lives. Far too many Christians have allowed the world to dictate to us how we should act, give, live, etc. We must abort this worldly mentally and take on the mind of Christ staying focused or as the title suggests, maintaining focus on Him.

As stated, I have shared with you that we must focus once again on Jesus. He is the star, the showcase, and is the number One. He is the Almighty One, He is sovereign; He is the head of the church (His body of believers). He's the founder, He sets the rules, the perimeters, the pace and the path we should be on. The bride (His body) must live holy and realize our position in Him, we must realize who and whose we are. We need to focus on His function, His order and the work of the Lord. We must focus on getting people saved so that they may be born again, repenting of their sins and coming into fellowship with Jesus allowing Him to be their personal Lord and savior.

I want to ask you two very personal questions. How many people have you witnessed to this week? Secondly, how many souls have you won to the Lord since you've been saved? The scripture in Proverbs 11:30 says, "the fruit of the righteous is a tree of life; and he that winneth souls is wise." This wise ministry of reconciliation is the heart of Jesus, for He came into the world to seek and save that which is lost, Luke 19:10. You will never be a soul winner if you are not focused on Jesus, His word and His work.

You might be thinking as you read that this writing sounds like another religious presentation or a boring time of hearing and reading the word of God. This will be a real conclusion to you unless your heart is moved in conviction to seek and see things from God's perspective. If you're not concerned with the things of God and only seeking to satisfy yourself, you will remain blind or blurred to the burden of God. A person with a selfish mindset will not and cannot focus and maintain on the things of God.

Chapter 1

Nehemiah 1:1-11
NEHEMIAH'S CARE AND CONCERN FOR THE CITY

Let's take a look at the text of Nehemiah chapter one in verse one. Nehemiah introduced himself with a bit of pedigree and gives the timing of his present situation. Nehemiah was a cupbearer to the king in the Shushan palace. Because of his position as cupbearer, he had a position of confidence and trust with the king. His responsibility as a cupbearer was to taste the king's wine to prevent him from being poisoned. He was a dedicated layman who was willing to give up the luxury of the palace to help his people. Jesus Christ is depicted in the book of Nehemiah as Jesus too was willing to leave His high position in order to identify with His people and give to the people the ministry of restoration.

Nehemiah's care of God's people and his care for the city of Jerusalem made him very concerned with what God was concerned with. He was concerned about God's heart so much that he was willing to put his life on the line for God. In verse two, Nehemiah inquired of his brethren who were left in Judah about God's work in Jerusalem. The report that he received was disappointing (verse three). The brethren explained that the remnants that were left in the city of Jerusalem are in great affliction and reproach since the walls of Jerusalem are now broken down and the gates are burned with fire. Jerusalem was the spiritual and political epicenter of Judah. Because of its condition, one could hardly see it as a city since it had no walls or gates.

In verse four, notice with me Nehemiah's heart reactions and concern to the news he received:

- He sat down - He stopped what he was doing. He was awestruck and had to be still.

- He wept - He was hurt over the fact that God's work was not being done.

- He mourned - He expressed grief. He lamented and was sorrowful at the condition of the people and the great city of Jerusalem.

- He fasted - He gave up eating voluntarily, withholding physical maintenance from himself. His concern and care for the city had caused him to fast from food.

- He prayed - He talked to God. He connected himself to God by conversing or dialoguing to Him.

Notice Nehemiah's prayer as he continues to pray from verses 5-11. The prayer reminded God of his covenant with His people. The prayer included confession of sin(s) verses six and seven. There was no covering up of the sins committed by God's people. Nehemiah realized that **"You can't hide from God anyway, be sure your sins will find you out!"** (Numbers 32:23). The prayer of Nehemiah reminded God again about the Word He gave to Moses in verses eight and nine. If they rebelled, God would scatter them. But if they returned, He would gather them. Nehemiah humbly asked God to hear his prayer on behalf of God's people.

He prayed that God would give him favor before the king where he was employed as the king's cupbearer. Nehemiah appealed to God based on His reputation among the heathens. Nehemiah did not want the heathens to think that He (God) was powerless to control and establish the people that

He had picked out to be His Chosen Ones. Caring and being concerned with what God is concerned with, will result in you being focused on Him and what He wants.

In verse 11, Nehemiah revealed something in his prayer that is essential for us if God will use us for His glory and that is the portion of scripture which says, "Who desire to fear thy name". **If you have no fear or reverence for God, you will go on doing your own thing not caring if you're focused on God's heart or His work.** Today, the trouble with too many Christians that are in the body of Christ is there is no reverential fear (a respect, an awe of God) in their hearts! That may be shocking to hear but nonetheless I believe it to be true. The major reason for a lack of reverential fear is the fact that the person may not know God; they may have met Him, but they don't know Him.

You can be introduced to a person knowing their name, where they are from, how tall they are, the color of their skin, hair and eyes, and their approximate weight and yet still not know the person, these are only facts about the person. You wouldn't necessarily know what makes them "tick" or what are the deepest desires of their hearts until you spend time with that person getting to know them on a personal basis.

If your heart is not right (right standing with God), you will never focus on Him and his work. Why would you concentrate on Him, and you don't know Him? How could you be FOCUSED on Him and His work when your heart is filled with other things? The scripture says in Proverbs 4:23, "Keep thy heart with all diligence for out of it are the issues of life."

Notice the wisdom Solomon continuously gives us in the following passages:

- Proverbs 4:24, "Put away from thee a froward mouth and perverse lips put far from thee." Watch how you use your tongue! This is expressing discipline of the tongue as God requires.

- Verse 25, "Let thine eyes look right on, and let thine eyelids look straight before thee," Watch what you allow your eyes to see! The eye gate is one way Satan can enter into your life.

- Verse 26, "Ponder the path of thy feet, and let thy ways be established" Be alert discern where you walk. You can't be focused walking any kind of way.

- Verse 27, "Turn not to the right hand nor to the left: remove thy foot from evil." Keep living holy and not live like the world. This is powerful wisdom from Solomon if we would be focused on the things of God; that is to be caring and concerned like Him.

God wants broken and contrite hearts (Psalm 51). Those are the hearts He can trust His anointing with as well as His glory and power. He wants men and women after His own heart so as to fill them with the most precious commodity there is and that is God himself. When we are filled with God, we will be God focused. We will be living God–inside minded. You don't beg and plead with focused people to worship, to work and to praise God. They realize this is what God created them for, to give Him pleasure and glory. He has become their life, their reason, and their purpose for living. These have His care and concern just like Nehemiah did.

The scripture says in psalms 122:1, "I was glad when they said unto me let us go into the house of the Lord." Are you glad (not sad) when it's time to assemble with the Body of Christ at your local fellowship? Do you ignore the prompting of the Holy Ghost as He impresses and reminds you it's time for church or do you gladly look forward to meeting Jesus and sharing warm fellowship with your brothers and sisters in the Lord?

In Hebrews 10:25 the scripture tells us not to forsake the assembling of ourselves together as believers in the Lord like others might do. There is a purpose for our coming together and that is to exalt and encourage each other in the Lord! You can't carry out "this" commandment if you are not in attendance when the saints gather.

Again, the scriptures declare in psalms 100:4 "I will enter into his courts with singing and thanksgiving in my heart; I will enter into his courts with praise." What kind of attitude do you possess when you come before the Lord, privately or publicly?

Psalms 34:1 reads, "I will bless the Lord at all times; His praise shall continually be in my mouth." Are you blessing Him or are you complaining and grumbling, blaming the Lord for the condition that you have found yourself in? This attitude clearly shows that you are not focusing on the Lord.

Psalm 42:1-2. "As the hart panteth after the water brooks, so panteth my soul after thee oh God-My soul thirsted for God, for the living God." Are you excited about God and the things He is concerned with?

Psalms 63:1, "Oh God, thou art my God **Early** will I seek thee, my soul thirsteth for thee. My flesh longeth for Thee in a dry and thirsty land where no water is."

You don't beg focused people to come to church and be on time, ready to worship and praise God. Just like the city of Jerusalem (a place), the Church is a place that God cares for. He built the church and professed that the gates of hell will not prevail against it. A caring, concerned focused person knows that he should be in the "place" and that while being there, it's a time that we minister unto Him.

You don't worry about **FOCUSED** people living in open immorality. Focused people don't live in the flesh desiring to live in fornication, adultery, lying, stealing, and gossiping and any other ungodly lifestyles. They don't have time or make

5

provisions for the flesh, no not for that! They don't have an interest in that sort of lifestyle! Their affections – emotions are set, fixed, and focused on things above not on things on the earth. For the focused person realizes his/her life is hidden with Christ in God. (Colossians 3:1)

Focused people with God's heart mortify their members which are upon the earth; fornication, uncleanness, inordinate affections, evil concupiscence, and covetousness which is idolatry. These things cause the wrath of God cometh on the children of disobedience. Nehemiah's example of being focused should encourage us to do what he did if we want the attention of God. He further shows us a man who cares and is concerned with what God is concerned with and willing to do whatever is necessary to bring glory and honor to God. Without a doubt, Nehemiah's heart was focused on what God's heart was focused upon and he showed it with his actions. He was sad because of the condition of the city but he was glad to serve God by leading in the completion of rebuilding Jerusalem's torn walls and gates.

Chapter 2

Nehemiah 2:1-20
WHEN YOU ARE FOCUSED YOU WILL RESPOND WITH ACTIONS

We should know that our hearts must be right with God if we would be focused on the things of God. We must present this kind of heart to God who is willing to fill it with himself. He is looking for the kind of hearts that are after His own heart. Hearts that are living God inside minded, hearts that are consumed with the concerns of God. Hearts that are focused on the things that God is pleased with and that will give Him pleasure.

Like David, a man after God's heart, the sweet psalmist and second king of Israel, Nehemiah is our example for this presentation of someone who had a heart after God, as someone who was concerned about what God was concerned with and willing to move in action to accomplish the assignment God has anointed for him to do. Nehemiah was someone who is focused on the things of God. When Nehemiah found out about the conditions of Jerusalem (the city of God) and its inhabitants, he responded with action.

As mentioned earlier in chapter one, he sat down- he stopped what he was doing. He wept- he was hurt over the fact that God's work was not being done. He mourned-he expressed grief. He lamented and was sorrowful. He fasted-he voluntarily gave up eating, withholding physical food maintenance from himself. He prayed -talked to God. He connected himself to God by conversing or dialoguing with

Him. He reminded God of the covenant that He had made with His people. He confessed his sins and the sins of the people. He made himself available in the hands of God as a servant to do something (he would take actions) regarding God's concern which was Jerusalem (the beloved city), her people and their plight.

There are people who say they want to do a work for God but that's about all; they just "say" they want to! Not everyone is willing to pray the price, pay the price, give the time, and the efforts it takes to follow God and to do what he says and be concerned with what He is concerned with. Not so with this servant. Nehemiah's concern lasted more than a Sunday or a week. He didn't just say a prayer about the situation that had caused him grief. Sadly, this is about as much concern as the average Christian displays toward the things of God. Nehemiah's actions were a great contrast to many of today's believers! He prayed over a period of four months from December to April!

Even though he was about 750 miles away from Jerusalem, he was praying to God on their behalf. He was in a place where he could have been enjoying the luxury and power in the palace of the king; instead, he committed himself to serious and desperate prayer. This is what would be expected of a focused person, someone who was concerned with what God was concerned with.

Nehemiah's concern caused him to pray. Prayer is the first action to be taken before you undertake a task for God. It has been said, "to be much for God, you must be much with God." You must get God's heart on any matter that He is concerned with. Nehemiah's prayer was not a quick few words, but rather he saturated himself in the presence of God so that he would get the right directions for this great task that was at hand. Nehemiah realized the importance of prayer. It is sad today that far too many of God's people see prayer as a chore and a duty and not as one of the most powerful weapons in our Christian arsenal.

Perhaps there are many who want to do a work for God and even started but were impatient and went to the battlefield without God's armor, direction or protection. This lack of concern and focus has caused the Christian defeat by the enemy, or they became weary in the warfare and abandoned the work of the Lord. Neither situation just presented is suitable for the focused saint!

Nehemiah was focused; he concentrated on what God wanted. He had a clear Image of what needed to be done. Even though he was loaded with this powerful insight, he also had the patience of God to move in God's timing. Oftentimes God will plant something in a person's heart, but the individual still must wait on God's timing before acting on that revelation. Four months had passed as Nehemiah was praying and seeking God's mind on how to help the people that he loved. God had given Nehemiah His plan, and now God was giving him His timing to go forth and share this revelation with the king.

When you are focused, boldness, faith and wisdom are some of the by-products that will be evident. Boldness was expressed when Nehemiah dared to go before the presence of the king with a sad countenance. The burden and sorrow that he felt for his beloved people in Jerusalem was upon him and there was no hiding of these emotions. In that day to go in the presence of the king with a sad countenance could have meant sure death for a person. Nehemiah's boldness was evident as he had been in the presence of the King of Kings and now, he proceeded into the presence of the king of the land to share what was in his heart.

Nehemiah expressed his faith as he believed that he could get an audience with the king. His faith believed that God would open the way for him. Proverbs 21:1 says, "The king's heart is in the hand of the Lord as the rivers of waters, He turneth it withsoever He will."

Nehemiah's presence was acknowledged by the king but before he responded to the king, wisdom kicked in insomuch as he prayed before telling the king his heart. In this case wisdom caused the cupbearer to get the protection and mind of God on how to tell the king about the burden that was burning in his bosom concerning his brethren in the beloved city of Jerusalem.

In verse five he shares his request or his desires to the king. In verse six, the king asks how long would his project take? Nehemiah gives the king a time reference. Verses 7 reveal the boldness, faith and favor of God was upon his life; he requests a letter, verse eight, to give him safe travel and guidance for his journey. Nehemiah also requests materials for the task at hand. In addition to giving him the letter and materials, verse nine tells us that the king sends captains of his army and horsemen with him for assurance and protection as he goes on his journey.

These verses let me know that God will make a way for us when we are set on doing His will and bidding. When our heart is about His business God will provide for our business. There is a saying that we are all familiar with, "where He guides, He will provide". This is definitely true in the case of Nehemiah. God provided spiritual guidance and everything naturally he needed to get the job done but Nehemiah's responsibility to God's generosity was to make himself available to the mission of rebuilding the walls and gates of Jerusalem.

In the realm of the Spirit, you must know that while God is "blessing", the devil starts "messing." In verse 10, Sanballat and Tobiah, the enemies of the children of God, heard that there was a man who had come to seek the welfare of the children of God. The devil and his demons seek to stop the progress of the people of God at every chance. The enemies of our faith don't want to see us healed and prospering or being successful in any area of our lives that we may give glory and praise to God for making these things happen for us.

Nehemiah was responding with action because he stayed focused on what God wanted in spite of the opposition. Once we know what God wants us to do, we must move expediently; however, we must move rightly (that is) in God's order. There was an order that Nehemiah had to go through. Even though he had vision, desire and fire, he had to follow proper channels. And when he followed order, the blessings of God followed him. Nehemiah did nothing for three days when he had come to Jerusalem. God's timing and patience is important for any successful work for God.

I pointed out earlier some of the by-products of being focused and as we look back at verse eight, we see the same endowments again. The scripture says that the hand of the Lord was upon focused Nehemiah. As a result, we continually see these spiritual tools being expressed in his life again. Boldness, faith and wisdom along with the favor of God caused him to move with confidence in the vision that he had regarding the welfare of the city of Jerusalem and her people.

Verses 12-15 indicate to us that it took about three months for Nehemiah to arrive at Jerusalem. Nehemiah operated in the wisdom of God once again. After arriving in Jerusalem, he was there three (days) before he did anything! You would have thought since he had such a burden for the city and the people there, he would have immediately begun working but wisdom and patience controlled him and allowed him to "be still." He may have appeared to have been silent but assuredly he was "still" moving in action by praying and seeking the mind and timing of God before undertaking this great work.

Wisdom and Patience wouldn't allow him to tell anybody what his plans were. He went out at night keeping counsel to himself. He was awake when others were sleeping and concerned when others were at ease. He saw more of the situation at night than others could see in the light! When you walk in the wisdom and patience of God, you will confuse the mind of your enemies!

In verse 16, it declares that Nehemiah didn't even chance sharing the vision and plans with those who would eventually help him do the work until he had surveyed and investigated the situation thoroughly. The "visionary" did not want well-meaning people to leak out the plans of God to the enemy until the correct timing of God was at hand.

After surveying the territory and the conditions of the city, Nehemiah was ready to share what God had placed in his heart to complete the work that God had assigned to him. Things will work out well when you follow the leadings of the spirit of God. God may begin in one person, but the ministry is not a one man show. The leader then must be able to communicate the vision to others accurately who will help in the work so that he that reads it will run with it according to Habakkuk chapter 2:2,3, "And the Lord answered me, and said, Write the vision, and make it plain upon tables, that he may run that readeth it. For the vision is yet for an appointed time, but at the end it shall speak, and not lie; though it tarry, wait for it, because it will surely come, it will not tarry."

Because he was focused, Nehemiah was able to encourage others to get focused and put their resources together and carry out the work/vision of God. If the leader is not focused and willing to move in actions, it is very doubtful that he will be able to motivate anyone else concerning the things of God. The leader cannot expect the helpers to be excited if he is not excited with an expected end.

In verses 17-18 Nehemiah challenged the leaders among the remnants to work with him (not for him) in repairing the walls. The motive behind the actions is "that we would be no more a reproach." Nehemiah understood that the people would be a reproach when they were not experiencing the glory of God, when they were not receiving the grace and power of God, when they were not walking in boldness, faith and wisdom. They would be a reproach when the enemies are\were making fun of them, their relationship with God and they are\were powerless to do anything about it. They are a reproach when God's name is not being honored among the heathens and are haters of God and yet the people of God remain silent!

This kind of reproach was not limited to Israel alone, the same conditions make us a reproach as well in these modern biblical times. We, like Israel, must rise up and not be a reproach, rejected by society and disrespected by the same when the word of God says we are Kings and Priests, a Royal priesthood (at that) and a peculiar people that should show the praises of our God! (1 Peter 2:9-10) The Bible teaches us that we are "more than conquerors" Romans 8:37, and "the Lord shall make you the head and not the tail and thou shall be above only and not beneath." Deuteronomy 28:13. We are those that "no weapon formed against us will prosper." Isaiah 54:17.

Nehemiah gives an accurate assessment of the conditions of Jerusalem to the people. Isn't it interesting though, that he had to tell the people their condition and they were the ones experiencing the tragedy? Sometimes you can live in a situation so long that you become used to it, familiar with it and common to the situation and now settled for what you have and not expect to be any better because your sight is limited! You have become comfortable believing that there is no improvement for you, no forward advancements, and no promotions for you. When you have become a "settler" someone like a Nehemiah must come along to let you see where you are and encourage you to know God wants better and more for you, praise God!

Nehemiah did encourage his people to work with him and rebuild the walls of Jerusalem. He further tells them how the "hand of God" was upon him, anointing him to do the work that he is encouraging them to help him with. He also tells them that not only was God's favor upon him, but the favor of the king of the land was upon him as well.

When Nehemiah shared the vision from a focused heart, the people caught the vision and said, "let us rise up and build," Nehemiah 2:18. Now that the people were focused, they were ready to move in action! The people were so encouraged and strengthened after hearing Nehemiah's vision that they were ready to run with the vision he had given them despite the continued harassment of the enemies of focus.

In verse 19, the terrible triple terrorists in the persons of Sanballat, Tobiah and Geshem continued to scorn, to despise, to make fun of and make threats that the remnant's efforts to do the work of the Lord would constitute rebellion against the king of the land. The people of God were focused as well as their fearless faithful leader. Nehemiah responded to the "triplets" in verses 20, by stating and exhibiting his faith in the God of heaven as One who would prosper them in their efforts for His glory. Nehemiah then counteracted the words of the terrorists by saying he and the servants of God would rise up and build.

Those who were not a part of the covenant of Israel would not have any part in the work of God. The fact that the enemies did not have a part in the work of God to control it and perhaps to take the glory for it, probably caused them to be angry and jealous. They showed their demonic disapproval and dismay through their continued harassment, ridicule and criticism.

O' that God would place and give more strong focused men and women to our local ministries who are focused on the vision of that assembly by the visionary and would rise-up with the man or woman of God in that house and say we will rise up and build and help you carry out the vision that God has placed in your heart for His glory and His honor.

Our houses of worship would be a beacon of light for the Lord in this darkened world. God is more than able to repeat Himself again in the lives of men and women who desire to please Him in a work that would glorify Him. Focused people will respond in action as they understand the will of God.

Chapter 3

WHEN WE ARE FOCUSED ON THE VISION OF THE LORD, WE WILL WORK AS ONE TO COMPLETE HIS WORK

In this third chapter of Nehemiah, you will find where the people of God were actually building the walls that had been destroyed earlier. Allow me to digress to share a little history before moving forward in this narrative. Before Nehemiah came to Jerusalem with the desire\fire from God to do this work, the prophet\priest Ezra had been permitted to return to Jerusalem from the Babylonian captivity of 70 years.

With the blessings of the king and as a byproduct he begins to rebuild the walls that had been down some 70 years earlier. When the enemies, the adversaries of Judah and Benjamin, were not allowed to help build, their wrath was stirred. They weakened the hands of the people and troubled them in building.

Men by the names of Rehum and Shimshai wrath was provoked so much so that they wrote letters back to the king telling him things that were not true regarding the building program and its motives. In response to the information the king commanded the work to be stopped until a further decree is issued.

When Rehum and Shimshai received the decree from the king, they hurried to Jerusalem and made them cease the work by force and power. They broke down the walls and burned the gates. This was the condition of Jerusalem when Nehemiah got the news. There had been between 15-16 years when no work was being done on the walls and gates of Jerusalem.

In review, we know that through his kinsmen, Nehemiah had learned the state of affairs and conditions that existed in Jerusalem. He was moved with heartfelt convictions and compassion for the heart of God. He stopped, he cried, he mourned, fasted and prayed for four months. He got his heart right with God because he wanted the heart of God on the matter. He was concerned with what God was concerned with.

Moving forward, Nehemiah was allowed to go before the king at the proper time. He received the king's blessings and the favor of God to do what God wanted to accomplish in him. Nehemiah used wisdom in his approach to begin the work and God honored him and caused him to have favor and the cooperation of the people as he shared God's vision to them.

As we now come to this 3rd chapter, we begin to see how those who would fit into the work of the vision. These individuals began to do the actual work, working together as one man. It was now time to work; no more talking, no more theorizing, no more summarizing, no more hoping and wondering about the conditions of the beloved city, it was time to work. Wherein timing and patience is needed in starting a work for the Lord, there comes a time when it is time to work! The people were focused, they had the vision, they knew what to do and they had a focused leader who could hear from God and God had equipped them with the necessary materials to do the work He had initiated.

The walls were high and very thick. They went for miles in some directions and in the various walls were gates where different kinds of activity took place. It was behind these walls and gates that the Temple and their houses were located which would be rebuilt as well. In building the walls and gates, it gave the people a sense of belonging, purpose, meaning and national community unity. These walls and gates had to be built.

As we explore this chapter from verses 1 through 32, you will notice that there are recorded at least 41 focused participants and their families who were rebuilding the walls and gates of Jerusalem under the focused leadership of Nehemiah. The one thing that they all had in common was to rebuild the walls and gates. They were focused as one to get this work completed. In completing the walls and gates there would no longer be a reproach among them. Because of their focus and unity, they worked together as one to carry out the vision of God which in reality would be helping themselves.

God did not need walls and gates to be God! No enemy could overthrow or overtake Him. He was no less God for all the years of their captivity even when and while the city of Jerusalem lay in ruins. No, what He was causing to be done was for their good. God is always looking out for the good of His people even when the enemy means it for evil, God can and will use the evil and make it good for us if we focus our attention on Him.

The walls and gates were being built. The scriptures share with us that there are at least seven walls mentioned and no less than 10 gates that were being built and or repaired. This speaks to the fact that even though they were focused and worked as one, various workers had different jobs to do. For example, not everyone built or repaired the sheep gate, the fish gate, the old gate, the valley gate, dung gate, water gate, fountain gate, the horse gate, the east gate or the gate Miph'-Kad. Different ones worked on various gates. What's important though is they were all working together for the good of all because they were focused on the same things.

The Gates

Each gate I believe had significance to the nation of Israel. It was important that the gates be rebuilt. With this thought in mind, I want to suggest to the reader that not only were the gates important to the nation of Israel but there are some "spiritual" lessons to be discovered for the New Testament Christian as we take a look at each gate in the text.

- Sheep gate-This may speak of Jesus Christ's sacrifice on the cross. This was the first gate repaired. The scriptures declare to us that without the sacrifice of Jesus as the "lamb slain before the foundation of the world", there would be no salvation. The other gates had locks and bars on them but none on this gate. For the door of salvation is open to all sinners. This was the only gate sanctified (set apart) as special.
- Fish Gate (vs. 3) Jesus called us to be fishers of men souls. For the New Testament Christian this gate could represent soul winning.
- Old Gate (vs. 6-12) this gate may speak of the old paths and truths of the word of God. People are looking for something new and they refuse to stay with the old truths that have been tested and have worked.
- Valley Gate (vs. 13) may remind the believer of the humility of Jesus. We too must humble ourselves before the mighty hand of God. Those that would humble themselves, will be exalted by God in due season.
- Dung Gate (vs. 14) waste and refuse of the city was taken here. This gate may speak of the cleansing of

our lives and teaching us about holiness and holy living.

- Fountain Gate (vs. 15-25) this gate may illustrate the ministry of the Holy Ghost. As New Testament believers, we need the Holy Ghost. When a person gets born again the Holy Spirit comes to live inside the believer. Without the spirit being present in the life of the believer, that person does not belong to God according to Romans chapter eight verses nine. When one is filled with the Holy Spirit and the Spirit is in charge, we as believers must take a back seat to His control.

- The Water Gate (vs. 26-27) may speak of the word of God which cleans the believer. The scripture says we are clean by the washing of the word of God.

- The Horse Gate (vs. 28) speaks of warfare. There are many battles the Christian will face as he journeys through this life.

- The East Gate (vs. 29) this gate may make us think of the second coming of Christ. Ezekiel saw the glory of God depart by the temple from the East gate. Later in Ezekiel 43:5, he saw the glory return from the way of the East.

- Gate Miphkad (vs. 31) speaks of God's judgment. In Hebrew the word means appointment, account and census. It carries the idea of troops showing up for revival or an appointed place for a meeting. The day is coming when God is going to call souls up for judgment to give in account of how we lived before Him and if we carried out the assignment on our lives. The believer will stand at the Judgment Seat of Christ to determine our faithfulness and rewards that we will receive. This judgment is not to determine our salvation but rather our rewards. There will be a future judgment for all unsaved persons to condemn them to a lake of fire. These individuals had a chance to receive Jesus Christ as savior, but they refused through neglect or pure rejection.

These are the gates and walls that Nehemiah and his servant helpers built. I believe these gates and walls have spiritual significance for us New Testament believers, as I hope you have seen above.

What we remember earlier from this chapter, is that there were many members to do the work on the walls and gates, but they were acting as one body. There were several different areas of work to be performed, but all the work was working together for the good of all! They were focused, concentrated and there was cooperation. Everybody had work to do, they did their part so that there would not be a breach, a tear or a hole, in the wall.

One of the biggest problems we face today in the local body of Christ is that many members in that fellowship are not satisfied with their assignment from God. God has taught us from the book of First Corinthians chapter 12, that there are many members in the body of Christ, and He styled them as body parts. Our natural bodies are composed of more than just one organ or body part. Each organ and body parts have their own distinct function to play but each part is working together for the good of the whole body.

Sometimes a "foot" wants to be a "hand" and vice-versa. An "ear" wants to be an "eye" and once again vice-versa. Then there are further conflicts between the "foot" and "eye" and with the "ear." God has placed many members together to make up one body. Every member must seek God for the purpose that He has for that believer. And then, that believer must do what God has assigned for him or her to do. Each person must stay in their lane and not try to do someone else's work.

For many in the body of Christ it's like when Christmas comes around. At Christmas we unwrap our gifts and when we look at our gifts, we then sometimes become disappointed. We go and look at others' gifts and we want their gift. We want to exchange our gift for their gift. The same thing happens in the body of Christ. We open up the gift(s) God has given us, and we run to someone else to see what gifts that person has, and we want their gifts rather than being satisfied with what God has given us.

If we look at the gift(s) God has given us and we are unhappy with it, there is the temptation to think to ourselves that we can swap it for something else. This scenario may be the reason why many have lost their individual anointing because they are claiming to be what they are not. This person is trying to operate in an anointing they were not suited for. David would not use Saul's armor when he faced the giant Goliath because Saul's' armor was not designed for the shepherd boy.

The body of Christ must stop this madness of attempting to "gift" swapping and trading of the gifts God has bestowed upon each member. We have nothing to do with the giving of gifts, it's as He wills. First Corinthians 12:1-12, and verse 40 lets you know who is in charge of the giving of gifts. God/Holy Spirit knows what each one of our capabilities are and He gives gifts accordingly. If you don't have what you think you should, it's a good indication that God knew you could not handle that grace, that might be the reason you don't have it!

Some in the body of Christ think they know what they are to be doing in service for the Lord, but I submit, these individuals might need to take another trip back to the potter's house to see indeed what the potter has made them for. Each man or men or their families in this third chapter of Nehemiah, had specific work to do that brought about good; not confusion, chaos, or divisions. What each man or family contributed was for the good of all the people.

Let's not be like the horse and mule in Psalms 32:9 where it says "Do not be like the horse or like the mule, which has no understanding which must be harnessed with bits and bridles. The horse will run ahead and is impatient. A mule is stubborn and will barely move. One runs too fast and the other hardly runs at all. The horse will run out of anointing and into the flesh while the mule dies in the flesh. The mule is styled as one who does not want anything from God and doesn't want to work for God with God's people.

Now as a pastor and leader of a local body of Christ, If I can't have all sheep who will follow the Lord faithfully, then I would rather have horses in the fellowship than mules! Horses are going somewhere, and the leader has the potential of bringing those horses under control so that the work and vision of that local fellowship can succeed.

For the body of Christ, let us focus and maintain focus together on the vision God has given and the work will be done. God will give the provision for the vision. He will provide favor and will be pleased with the product. There will be no reproach, no breach, no one without work to do, and no one without purpose and meaning in their lives.

There will be co-operation and co-laboring. There will be unity of hearts and purpose because all moving parts will move/be in action going in the same direction with the same goals. This kind of selfless action will bring glory to God and not to ourselves. I believe it's time out for the individual superstars, and the mavericks who want to do their own thing.

We must move as one, act as one, to accomplish the vision or the goals that God has given. We can't or won't move as one until we get in order. When we have order we will get/have the anointing to do the work. Our collective efforts as one will make an impact on our families, our places of worship, our surroundings, our communities, our state and our nation.

Chapter 4

THE ENEMIES OF FOCUS WITHOUT AND HOW TO DEAL WITH THEM

There will always be enemies against the work, the ways, the will, the wisdom, the worship and the word of God.

There will never be a time on earth whereby the devil, the flesh and or the world will not try to hinder the Lord's work. These three, the world, the devil and the flesh are our ever-present enemies.

If the devil doesn't show up himself, he will send one of his representatives or he will deceive the believer to appeal to our flesh covering it with plenty of religious words. If this effort of his fails, he will try to induce a strong dose of the world's mentality to counteract the ways and the word of God. Either way(s) enemies are always present to hinder the work of the Lord.

I believe the genesis of keeping the enemy from stopping the work of God and thus hindering and destroying us as believers is-we must have our hearts right and focused on God. The enemies of God in some way or another will always try to stop the believer once he is committed (focused) and concentrated on and to God. The best way to defeat the enemy as he comes against you is to be "red hot" on fire for the Lord. A believer "on fire" for God will be difficult for the devil to handle. This believer, filled and be ye being full of the spirit of God according to Ephesians 5:18 and walking in an authority that he already possesses in the Lord, makes himself victorious over every attack of the enemy! Praise the Lord!

If you as a believer have said "YES" to God; that is an eternal YES, a once and for all YES, no matter what the cost; yes, no matter what the persecution; yes, no matter the trials; yes, or the tests; yes, you will be able to stand against the wiles of the devil and come out victorious! The apostle Paul lets us know in the book of Ephesians chapter six, that the devil has a wile (method) for every believer. Satan has been watching you like he did Peter to sift you.

The devil knows your weakness because he has been watching you as you live life each day. Satan throws his fiery darts at the believer, but the Bible assures us that our faith in the Lord will give us the victory over the devil's wiles anytime we exert faith. We have the victory that overcomes the world, even our faith. 1 John 5:4.

You and I are not much of a threat to the devil if we are not focused on Jesus! When our minds and hearts are focused on ourselves and or worldly pursuits, Satan has an entry to our lives. Remember from John's gospel chapter ten, the enemy comes to steal, kill and to destroy. A mind that is not set on things above where Christ sits on the right hand of the Father, will give the enemy a chance to invade our lives and bring destruction. (Colossians 3:1-3).

However, when you are focused you become bold, you move in faith with a faith that pleases God, and you have the wisdom and the favor of God on your life.

In the book of Acts chapter 4, the enemies of Christ took note that the disciples of Jesus were bold and courageous. Their conclusion was these men had been with Jesus. If we spend time with the Lord, He will help us to be victorious over any situation and obstacles that we may face.

In chapter 2:10 and verses 19, We saw where Nehemiah had come to Jerusalem to rebuild the walls of that city that had been destroyed some seventy years earlier by the Babylonians. And approximately fifteen years before Nehemiah's rebuilding efforts, the partial rebuilding of the walls and gates by Ezra had been destroyed as well. Enemies of the rebuilding work of Nehemiah showed up in the presence of three men. These men were Sanballat, the Hornite, Tobiah, the servant and Geshem, the Arabian. They heard that Nehemiah had come to Jerusalem to rebuild its walls. I might add the devil always tries to listen to the plans of God given to His servants to complete! Be alerted that every assignment that God gives his servants, know this, that enemies will show up and try to discourage you in that work.

The devil will try to stop any assignment that God has given you in its infant stage before it gets off the ground. The enemy knows once the work gets some momentum and strength it will be even more difficult for him to win. Satan will often taunt the believer with words that he hopes will produce doubt and fear. The devil knows and we should know that when one gets over into fear, faith leaves thus there is no pleasing God and there will be no victory to experience.

"They laughed at us to scorn and despised us and said, what is this thing that ye do, will you rebel against the king? Nehemiah 2:19. Earlier work had been done on the wall during the time of Ezra the prophet but opposition to it halted the work claiming it was a revolt against the king. Nehemiah had sought to rebuild the walls some sixteen later for the real King of Kings!

The first attack of the enemy seemed to be ridicule, scorn, to make "sport" of, and to be looked upon with contempt. The enemy knows if he can break your confidence and help you to foster a spirit of inadequacy, you will feel defeated and will not pursue the work God has committed to you. Even though the devil will speak to our minds, he often uses other humans under his control to express these negative thoughts, producing a defeated attitude. Be careful not to allow the enemy of God to use you for his advantage to spoil the plans of God.

Again, in this chapter, one can see that the devil (in human form) is coming against Nehemiah and God's people in the presence of Sanballat as he hears that Nehemiah and Israel were building and repairing the torn walls and gates of Jerusalem. The enemy was angry and took great indignation and mocked the Jews. In verse two in this chapter four, Sanballat called others in with him to mock the people of God.

Sanballat called and mocked and ridiculed the people by saying they were feeble and weak Jews. He further mocked saying the work they were trying to do is more than they could do or handle. Continuing, Sanballat questioned how they could make a wall and gates from burned rubbish heaps? All of this ridicule and negative talk was to discourage the work of Nehemiah and the Jewish people.

In verse three, from another voice of opposition and that being the voice of Tobiah, who also tried to make fun of them. He suggested that if they built a wall and a fox climbed on top of it, the fox would break down their stone wall. The enemy never runs out of critics to the work of God.

Nehemiah becomes our example when this kind of warfare comes at us in our attempt to do God's work and to please Him. Nehemiah learned in the secret place of God that you don't fight the devil in your own strength. Nehemiah realized that the battle was the Lord, and the work was sure to be completed despite the ridicule of the enemies of God. This soldier, this leader knows that God is bigger than any devil that would show up to show out against them!

Nehemiah knew what we would later receive as a revelation through the apostle Paul's writings, "the weapons of our warfare are not carnal but mighty through God to the pulling down of strongholds bringing into captivity every imagination and high thought to the obedience to God." 2 Corinthians

10:4. God will work it out if we let Him! As a believer you can't fight these demons that come against the work of God with your mother's attitude or your father's will power. We must commit our ways to the Lord for the battle is the Lord's, hallelujah to our strong and powerful God!

Nehemiah's reaction to the taunts of the enemies and the fear found within the fellowship caused him to pray. Nehemiah didn't fight in the flesh; he carried his concerns to the Lord. He made the battle spiritual for we wrestle not against flesh and blood but principalities, powers, rulers of darkness and spiritual wickedness in high places, Ephesians 6:12.

Earlier in this chapter in verses four and five, when Nehemiah heard what his enemies had said, he sought the Lord in prayer. Because prayer is a spiritual weapon, he prays again, "hear, O our God; for we are despised and turn their reproach upon their own head and give them for a prey in the land of captivity: And cover not their iniquity and let not their sin be blotted out from before thee: for they have provoked thee to anger before the builders." As the opposition and ridicule intensifies, he prays again in verse nine allowing God to be the solution to their situation. Nehemiah set a watch day and night against the enemies of focus. We too must watch and pray, so says the word of God!

The man or woman who is shallow in prayer, will be shallow in their productions for the Lord. The person who touches God in prayer, touches the heart of the people who hears that prayer. So, we must pray with purpose, power, passion and pleadings. We get power, wisdom and directions when we pray.

The world will never believe in a religion where there is no power and demonstration of that power. A rationalized faith, a social church, a moralized gospel may gain the applause of man, but these things awaken no convictions and win no converts. If we are going to be much for God-we must be much with God through prayer. Nehemiah's life exemplified a life committed to prayer.

When you commit your ways to the Lord in prayer you become focused. Your concentrated mind is made up to follow God as you have fortified yourself in Him. The devil knows that it's hard to move you and get you to come off the wall when you are focused!

So, know that each time you don't move from your assignment(s) from God, the devil will intensify his strength and tactics against you to destroy you and make you quit the work of God. Remember what Nehemiah knew and did, he understood the battle is the Lords and through prayer he would be victorious. Don't get in fear and don't come off your faith, God will fight our battles! God brought them through one test, but how many know that the devil doesn't stop because you've gained one victory?

Notice how Nehemiah stayed focused and the advancement of the work of the Lord continued. In verse six it says, "So built we the wall; and all the wall was joined together unto the half thereof; for the people had a mind to work." Now, notice the evil progression of the enemies of focus because when Sanballat first heard of the work that Nehemiah was doing, he was grieved. Sanballat now vamped his attack and began to laugh at the work God gave Nehemiah to accomplish.

From this state of opposition, Sanballat moved to anger and then mocked the Jews. He also ridicules and belittles the people of God. Sanballat's anger is ratcheted yet further as we see in verses seven and eight. He is very wroth; very angry. He calls out to others to get in agreement with him to fight against the work of God since the work now was well underway.

Why would Sanballat fight Nehemiah and the Jews? It simply was because Nehemiah and the Jews wanted to obey and please their God. The enemies of focus don't want God's body to obey Him and be built up. The enemies of God will always seek to destroy God's people, their plans and their progress. If you seek to obey God, you will have opposition. Jealousy and envy become tools of opposition in the hands of the enemy. Stay focused, people of God and give Him thanks. You would not be receiving this level of warfare that is coming against you if what you are doing was not bringing glory to God!

The believer must remain focused on the assignment(s) of God and not allow the taunts/threats of the enemy to discourage them. Satan will use anyone at his disposal to stop the work of God. The people/leaders of Judah begin to allow the voices of the enemy to hinder and halt them in their efforts to please the Lord. When disunity and discouragement happen within the fellowship, it makes the task at hand more difficult to accomplish.

In verses 10-12, the voices of the enemies caused some of the Israelites leaders to be discouraged so they would not build. The leaders/workers began to complain saying they did not have much strength and there was too much rubbish to work through and they would not be able to build. The leaders/workers begin to get in fear rehearsing what the enemy had said and what they were going to do to them; to kill them, so the work would cease.

The believers/servants of God cannot rehearse mutter - (to say over and over) what the enemy is saying to you and about you - and you still walk in victory. They repeated what the enemy had said to them at least ten times. This repetitiveness is more than enough times to get this negative image of defeat in their spirit. You have got to change those words that the devils hurl at you with the word of God. Say what God has already said. The Bible encourages us in the book of Romans chapter twelve, to renew our mind with the word of God. Let us learn to say what God says only!

If God has given you a word and a work, stay focused on what He said. Speak only what God said and not get in agreement with the enemy to abort what God said and assigned for you to complete. Our positive confessions of God's words are vital to our success in the Lord. Let's discipline our mouths and our minds and get in agreement with what God says.

Joshua 1:8 reminds us to not allow the word of God to depart from our mouths. The verse says," This book of the law shall not depart out of thy mouth; but thou shalt meditate therein day and night, that thou mayest observe to do according to all that is written therein; for then thou shalt make thy way prosperous, and then thou shalt have good success." We are assured victory and success if we stay with and say what God says.

The remnants of Israel or any other local assembly should thank God for a focused leader with a vision from God. Nehemiah, and hopefully your leader knows the voice of God as well as knowing the voice of the devil. If you know both voices, knowing the difference between the two, you will never ever have to be worried about defeats in our lives, especially if we follow the voice of the shepherd of our souls and not a stranger (the devil).

Nehemiah used the God given wisdom that he possessed. Watch the actions and listen to what Nehemiah did and said in verse 13-14 as he heard all the treats and harassment from the enemy. He even heard thoughts of doubt and unbelief being expressed to him by the people that should be in agreement with the work of rebuilding the walls and gates of Jerusalem.

From a natural position, Nehemiah strategically placed armored men/families at the most vulnerable places (lowest points) on the wall so as to be on the lookout for invading enemies. From a natural posture, Nehemiah now moves to a spiritual strategic point when he reminds the people to "be not afraid of them; remember the Lord which is great and terrible, and fight for your brethren, your sons, and your daughters, your wives, and your houses."

Nehemiah insisted that the people be not afraid of their enemies, that the Lord alone is to be feared. Nehemiah changed the narrative and got the battle over into the spiritual realm knowing that God would fight their battle with and for them. The enemies wanted the people to be afraid, to be discouraged, to be troubled, to be confused, to be disturbed and come out of their faith. Nehemiah changed the words of the enemy to faith affirmations.

The result of this strategy is noted in verses 15, the enemy's plot was plundered and became powerless. God had brought their plots to naught; He exposed the enemy, and He confused their counsel. The work of the Lord was continued as all the workers returned to the wall and resumed the work. The Lord came through for them once again and He will do the same for us as well! The wisdom that God had deposited in Nehemiah continued to display itself in the actions of this great man of God. The warrior knew his assignment was to build but he also knew he had to battle!

In verses 16-22, the cupbearer now turned military strategist, strategically implored the workers to become potential soldiers as well. While working each man had "strapped" himself with a sword, shield or spear or bow in the event of an invasion of the enemy. They "stayed dressed" for an emergency as they did not remove their clothes, verse 23, except only to wash them at the water.

With one hand they worked on the wall and the other hand was occupied with a weapon. The people were encouraged to spend the night inside of the city of Jerusalem for mutual protection. The people were separated from each other along the wall so, a trumpeter stayed near Nehemiah to sound an alarm if needed to gather all the people together in one place as the work was extensive and spread out.

Know this, the people of God, who are focused on pleasing Him, will be confronted by those who do not want the work of God to be productively successful. Nehemiah confronted his enemies with prayer, faith and godly wisdom and defeated them each time they came against him and the work he was doing for God.

We too will have our Sanballats, the Hornites, the Tobiahs, the servant and Geshem, and the Arabian to hinder and attempt to halt us from the work of God. But let us take the example of Nehemiah's actions of wisdom, prayer, courage and faith and we too will watch God give us victories over the enemy like He did with Israel and Nehemiah.

Chapter 5

Nehemiah 5:1-13

THE ENEMIES OF FOCUS WITHIN AND HOW THEY MUST BE DEALT WITH

In the last presentation, we saw how Nehemiah dealt with the enemies from without and how he defeated them soundly. Now we see him dealing with the enemies of focus from within. One thing that must be said of Nehemiah is that he was focused on what God wanted. He had the heart of God, and that heart was for God. This is of utmost importance if we would be used of God for His glory and honor.

One's heart must be right with God. As a believer, we must allow God to perform spiritual surgery on us to cut out, heal, mend and sew up our wounded heart so that nothing is in our heart that will keep God from working through us. God must have access to any and all areas of our hearts that may be too painful for us to let anyone else see it. Yet, the Great Physician wants to get to the very "heart of the matter."

When our hearts are right with God, He can trust us with greater assignments for His glory. Nehemiah's heart was focused and right with God. A person whose heart is not right with God can go through the motion of ministry without truly being used by God. We can preach with emotions or talents, but that does not mean what he/she is doing is anointed of God. A person can go through motions of ministry, but God is not receiving any glory out of the efforts. A person may well be successful in society but that does not mean he was successful with God. We can be busy but barren!

Many in the body of Christ are trying to produce fruit without having the seed from God for that fruit. The womb of their hearts is not right with God. Spiritually speaking many want babies but have not conceived because their womb (heart) is unhealthy, and it can't conceive.

A healthy heart will make it possible to conceive. In order to have births (fruit, productivity, successes) there has got to be some intimacy, then conception, travail and ultimately birth. Many are trying to give birth but have not been intimate with God that He may plant His divine seed in them during intimacy and conception.

Some Christian servants are looking at other servants who seem to stay in the "spiritual maternity ward" birthing babies one after another. Some are producing multiple births, twins, triplets, sextuplets, etc. Others are pushing hard trying to give birth but there is no seed in them; there is no conception. Therefore, one cannot birth/produce that "holy thing."

From the look of much of our fruit, we have not been intimate with God but rather have been intimate/laying with the devil! Oops, probably shouldn't have said that! But nevertheless, I believe we are producing fruits that look more like the devil than looking like spiritual babies or fruits from the seed of God! The scriptures in Luke 6:43-45 teaches us that a tree is known by the fruits it bears. The man or woman that is "good" (a good heart) according to this scripture, brings forth good; and an evil man/woman out of the evil treasure of his/her heart brings forth evil.

Have we forgotten that we are to be conformed into the image of Jesus in II Corinthians 3:18? Jesus is on display for us to see Him, to contemplate His glory and we are supposed to be transformed into His image from glory to glory. Our fruits, efforts, our spiritual babies ought to look like godly fruits. The church should be pregnant with passionate propagation where she is often pleading for pure production.

There must be intimacy with the Lord. We must spend time with Him and allow Him to have His way with us, then there will be conception and birth. Even after conception there will be travail and labor pains. But when these pains are experienced, you know you got something in you! Yet still, there are those who got the seed of God in them but have allowed the enemy to help them abort that seed. This individual may then go about thinking they are carrying seed but only "hot air."

Saul and Samson are both examples of this scenario. In the case of Samson who had been given incredible strength by God to defeat the enemies of God's people. There was a secret to his power, and he was never to divulge where that strength lies. Samson flirted with an enemy girl. His heart lost focus on his mission. Samson revealed the source of his strength to her. He was captured by his enemies, and he thought he still had the power on his life as he once had. Samson was rudely surprised; his power was now gone. The enemy had caused him from "within" to lose the power that he once possessed. Samson's power was needed for those enemies of God outside Israel's covenant, but now, the power was gone.

Saul, the first king of Israel, disobeyed God and lost his anointing and position as king, yet he continued to operate in that position. Saul had allowed the devil to work from "within" and entered his heart with greed, fear and selfishness to defeat him. The devil helped him to lose what God had bestowed upon him.

Why all the talk about the heart? When the heart is not right with God, negative production is a result. The person whose heart is not right with God does not care who he hurts as long as it benefits them. They are unconcerned about the plight of the marginalized or those less fortunate. The hearts of many of those in Jerusalem at the time of Nehemiah revealed what was really in them.

God had given these people victory over their enemies who were "without" but now they have become enemies to their kinsmen "within." You must stay focused on what God has given and protect the anointing and guarding the seed that has been planted inside you.

The need here is to re-focus since these once focused people have forgotten where they had come from. You've got to know that there will be those enemies that would seek to and help you abort what God has put in you. Your conception has got to be from God, because in the spirit you don't get yourself pregnant!

Once Nehemiah got the seed of God's word for the work of God, he met opposition from without through Sanballat, Tobiah and Gresham. These three all tried to get Nehemiah to abort the "baby" (the work) or have a premature birth (don't finish the work properly). These were enemies/forces "without" to hinder, slow down or stop the work of God. The enemies' strategies did not work. With prayer to God, that is, staying intimate with Him, being focused on God, Nehemiah and the remnant Jews had the courage to fight off the enemy tactics and devices to steal, kill and to destroy what they were doing for the Lord.

Nehemiah and his people prayed and watched with a working instrument in one hand and a sword in the other. They continued to carry out the vision that God had given to Nehemiah. This was one battle won, one victory in the fight, but we must not get so comfortable, be at ease and relax in Zion! Why? Because the enemy is yet plotting his next move. He will not stop at the first sign of his defeat.

The enemy is still looking for opportunities to do his ungodly work. When the enemy cannot defeat you from "without", he will try to defeat you from "within". If the enemy can't get you to go back to the clubs after God has delivered you or get you to drink the devil's brew or use drugs again, he will try to stop you from "within" with some other kind of satanic strategies. Satan tries and is often successful on many occasions to get the body of Christ/the local congregations to turn on one another.

Notice this, that even though Sanballat and the rest of the enemies of focus attempted to defeat the Jews from "without", the work of the Lord continued. However, when there was strife, selfishness, greediness, division and contentions from within, there was no work on the walls, or the gates done in this chapter!

The body of Christ has got to come together if we will progress in the work of the Lord. As Nehemiah was focused on obeying God, he was blessed. But Nehemiah had to model these characteristics and preach to the Jews in order to get the work done. He had to organize and strategize their efforts in unity as their enemies wanted disunity.

From verses one to five of this chapter, there came a "cry from within" the body (men and women) against their own brethren. An economic crisis was taking place where the poor among the people found it difficult to buy food and other resources to maintain their families. A lesson to be learned at this point is, just because you're doing a work for the Lord does not mean you want to be met with challenges and obstacles.

The heartless noble Jews were extorting and taking away from other marginalized and financially depleted Jews. These heartless Jews were charging their brothers "much" for food along with absorbent interests. In addition to the high prices charged for food and interests to be paid, these struggling Jews also had to borrow money to pay their taxes to the Persian King. Jewish noblemen and the rich few were putting their own brethren's children in bondage.

The parents did not have the money to redeem their children. Others had taken their lands, olives yards and vineyards. Satan was now causing trouble from "within". Satan was defeated from "without" with wisdom that God had given Nehemiah, but now he (Satan) moves to another tactic to cause division and disunity from "within".

Isn't that just like the devil if he can't defeat you one way he is not going to stop there? Want he try another way? Galatians 5:14-15 says, "For all the law is fulfilled in one word, even in this; Thou shalt love thy neighbor as thyself, but if ye bite and devour one another; take heed that ye be not consumed one of another."

Today, we have this revelation of loving one another in the New Testament, but there is no reason to believe that the Jews of Nehemiah's time did not know to love one another as well. The above scripture further seems to give a word picture of two wild carnivorous animals furiously fighting, biting and eating each other as to devour one another. This scenario is applied to the Jews as some brothers were now destroying their own ancestral relatives. They were eating up their neighbors' goods, vexing them, hurting them and bringing destruction to their lives.

When we turn on each other in the body of Christ, we become a weakened body and when we are weak; we are not strong. We become a suspicious body, we begin to devour one another, and no one is getting the glory out of that situation but the devil. The work of God will stop when there is no real love shown. What is often shown; however, is an emotion that is expressed in greed and selfishness. When this happens, the vision for the people will be on hold and no "spiritual babies" will be born in the womb of that environment.

The enemy gets a chance to re-group and hit us while we are operating on his turf. In the flesh, individuals have opened themselves up for an invasion from the enemy. There will always be disunity, dishonoring and division when we don't love and submit to the Lordship of Jesus Christ. When one submits to His lordship, we will love one another, we will get in spiritual order and follow spiritual leadership.

Verse six shares with us that Nehemiah heard the news of the crisis from his abused and exploited brethren, consequently, he was very angry. One might say "the man of God, the leader, the visionary should never get angry." Really? The New Testament book of Ephesians 4:26, teaches us to be angry but sin not. Sometimes it becomes necessary to express indignation against social injustice. This is exactly what Nehemiah did.

I wonder where are the voices today that would speak out for those who are marginalized and are treated unjustly? In Matthew 21:12, Jesus expressed righteous anger and indignation when He cleared the temple courts as many money changers were selling their wares in the temple while exploiting the people. Nehemiah had the heart of God. He was angry over the fact that the Jews were allowing Satan to use them in dealing so wrongly with their brethren.

From verse seven, we see where Nehemiah consulted with himself. He thinks about the situation that was before him and I'm sure he also prayed. From his meditation, he decided to and does rebuke the nobles and rulers regarding their unscrupulous actions. These men were those who were being used by the devil against their own countrymen. He chided them by telling them they were extracting interest from their kinsmen and therefore acting just like the heathens around them.

This effort was certainly warranted but he also called a "church meeting" to further make his point. This issue of exploitation among some fellow countrymen had to be addressed before the work at hand of building the walls and gates could/would proceed. Like Nehemiah, the leader of any group, church or an organization must be ready to confront any enemy that comes against God's work.

In verse eight, Nehemiah continues to explain and remind his audience that their brothers were once sold and then redeemed by God but now they should not be sold even unto another Jew. The noble's actions were unprofitable to the body of the now landless landowners Jews among them. As Nehemiah continues his rebuke, the guilt that the nobles experienced was so deep and obvious, that they had no rebuttal or excuse.

Verse nine, give somewhat of an additional clue as to why the nobles were committing this kind of atrocity against their brethren. Nehemiah tells them that they should "walk in the fear of the Lord" which would avoid reproach among the Gentile enemies. Is this not the reason why we commit acts that we know are against the expressed will of God? The fear of God is often missing in our lives. I'm suggesting here a reverential fear, a respectful fear that honors and expresses an "awe" to and for the Lord.

When an individual aligns himself with other believers and he is hurting them by his actions with no remorse for what he is doing, this is a good indication that there is no fear of God in their lives. With this kind of behavior, there certainly seems to be no concern for their brother(s). In the case of a Christian who behaves negatively toward another Christian, that negative person does not realize or seem to care that he is also affecting unbelievers. This negative action may hinder the unsaved from ever being a part of the body of Christ.

Nehemiah tells the nobles in verse 10, that he, his household and his personal servants are lending money and grain to the people but without interest. He gives forceful godly counsel and tells the nobles to leave off the interest, at once, that they were charging the people.

In verse 11, he tells them to restore (give back) what they had taken from their brethren. The list included their fields, vineyards, olive groves and houses. The command also includes the noble giving back a portion of the interest that they had gained from the people.

If you are allowing the devil to use you in bringing about ungodly divisions, and if you are hurting your brethren, God is calling you to a place of repentance. There needs to be a change immediately from that kind of behavior. This behavior is not productive for the body of believers nor is it edifying. It does not glorify God. It is producing negative results and it's not good neither is it of God.

Often when a person has rebelled and has been rebuked publicly, they either continue to rebel and fight or they try to blame someone else for their evil selfish greedy actions. But thank God that when these rebels were rebuked by the man of God, they repented and received corrections and instructions from him. As evidence of their repentance, the nobles said in verse 12, we will give all we took back to our brothers and not demand anything more from them. They said in essence, Nehemiah, we will do what you say.

In verses 12b, Nehemiah realized that sometimes talk is cheap. So, the man of wisdom and authority called the priest to witness an oath that he made the nobles and officials declare that they would do what they had promised regarding their restoration efforts to their brothers. After the rebuke, the repentance and the restoration, the corrections and instructions, in verse 13, Nehemiah does something that may be strange to our culture. He shakes the lap of his robe in a gesture to symbolize the solemnity of the oath that was taken by the nobles and officials. The act was to reinforce the fact that there would be curses; serious consequences, if the oath was not fulfilled by them. Nehemiah shook his robe and asked God to "shake- out"- "empty out" any person among them who would not restore what they had taken from their fellow countrymen. Nehemiah wanted God to deal severely with those who would not do what they had made oaths to do. He wanted them exposed and emptied!

In the New Testament book of Matthew 10:14, Jesus told His disciples to perform a strange act after preaching and under certain conditions, which may be foreign to our culture. He tells them to "shake the dust off their feet" after they had preached the gospel to the people and they nor their message was not received by the hearers. The shaking of dust off their feet was a testimony against those rejectors. Shaking the dust symbolized that one has done all that can be done in a situation and therefore carries no further responsibility for it. The disciples could walk away with a clear conscience knowing they had done all that they could.

Also, in the New Testament book of Acts chapters 13 and 18, Paul shook the dust off his feet when the gospel message he and his fellow workers were preaching was rejected. Paul had put Jesus's words into practice. The symbolic act of shaking the dust from one's feet was a warning to the regions that they preached in, and the message and messenger was rejected. Paul and his missionary entourage held no further responsibility for the people's level of acceptance to the gospel message. In all three cases, with Nehemiah, the disciples and Paul, the hearers were exposed to the truth, so the messengers were not held guilty of their blood if the people did not repent.

When we are focused or have the need to refocus on Jesus and the task(s) He has given us, we must remember to watch and pray lest we enter into temptation of the devil. The enemy would love to stop the work of God, hinder it, put it on hold, defeat it or to destroy it at any cost. Those enemies of focus "without or within" must be dealt with. We must maintain focus and keep the vision alive and complete the assignment that God has given us for His glory!

Chapter 6

Nehemiah 5:14-19

FOCUSED PEOPLE GIVE OF THEIR SUBSTANCES AND POSSESSIONS TO THE WORK OF GOD

The emphasis of this message is, when you are focused on the Lord, not only do you give yourself to God for His service and glory, but you give your substances, your possessions and resources to the work of God. Looking back to the previous thirteen verses of this chapter, we saw that the enemy of focus tried to ambush, abort and annihilate the vision of God that was being carried out under the leadership of Nehemiah and these post-exilic Jews. The enemy of focus came from within and from without. In both cases proper adjustment was made. The man of God corrected his fellow countrymen who were abusing their own. Nehemiah and his people rejected the advancements of Sanballat and his crew and kept on building.

The man of God got God's wisdom and put a trowel in one hand and a sword in the other and kept on working. Nehemiah openly rebuked the Jews that were profiting from their countrymen. These noblemen were putting their kinsmen in bondage, taxing and charging interest on those less fortunate. The noblemen repented and restored stolen possessions to their family members.

Nehemiah and his people refocused/maintained focus and didn't allow the enemy to destroy what God had started through this godly yielded man. When we are focused and doing work for the Lord, we must always watch and pray as the scriptures suggest; "Be sober and vigilant because your adversary the devil is seeking to whom he may devour" I Peter 5:8.

The devil is constantly looking for inroads to destroy the work of God as well as destroying our lives. The devil tactics and devices are evil and deceptive. If the enemy cannot get you one way, he will seek, search, say, and suggest anything to get us out of focus and out of the will of God.

In this text, you will see Nehemiah's unselfish example of using his resources in the work of God. He was focused and as a result, giving was no problem for him. One must understand that if the enemy can get you to become stingy and selfish with anything God has given you, then he has a foothold in your life. The devil will use your selfishness and greediness to keep you out of the perfect will of God.

God has given us many abilities, talents, treasures, giftings and anointings. If you are selfish and stingy with these giftings and not use them for the glory of God, Satan gains a place in your life, and he hurriedly seeks to develop a stronghold in that area of your life to thwart your usability with and for God. What is it Christian that you are stingy and selfish with, that God has given you for His work and you won't use it or give it for His glory? God's gift to us is not for our egos and for building our empires nor is it given for us to "strut your stuff."

It is obvious in the text that God had blessed Nehemiah tremendously. He was a wealthy man but a humble man and a giving man. You have heard it said before and it's worth repeating, "if God can get it through you, He will give it to you." History reports that Nehemiah came from a well to do family of Jews living in Shushan. His position as a cupbearer to the king was also lucrative. He was a man of wealth and distinction. Did you know God blesses us so that we can be a blessing? For those who have been blessed by God in any abundance (not just money), you ought to be willing to be rich toward God in good works.

According to I Timothy 6:17-19, it says, "Charge them that are rich in this world, that they be not high-minded, nor trust in uncertain riches, but in the living God, who giveth us richly all things to enjoy", vs. 18, "That they do good, that they be rich in good works, ready to distribute, willing to communicate", vs. 19,"Laying up in store for themselves a good foundation against the time to come, that they may lay hold on eternal life." Nehemiah's life and actions personified these passages on all levels.

Nehemiah was appointed governor of Judah under the reign of King Artaxerxes. Nehemiah's appointment as governor coincided with the king's reign from the twentieth year unto the thirty second year of his rule, verse 14. This time period is significant as you consider the rest of the verse. Nehemiah states that for these twelve years serving as governor, he nor his kin ate the food allowed to him as governor. If we modernize his statement, Nehemiah was saying he took no salary from his position as governor. He had a right to a salary, but he did not receive one.

This is amazing and it tells me that he was sufficient, he had wealth and had no need to take any salary nor resources due to him because of his position. Previous governors, in verse 15, had taken a large salary in silver and was chargeable to the people in addition to taking food and wine from them.

There was nothing wrong with the people taking care of the governor. Much like the church taking care of a pastor and the staff of a local church ministry. One of the reasons Nehemiah said he did not take a salary or lord his position over the people was because of the fear of God in his life!

The reverent fear, the awe and the respect of God is missing in the life of a lot of believers. Why do we know? We have only to look at their behavior, a behavior that is in direct opposition to God's position; and that is His truth! When we find ourselves abusing and misusing others, it's a sure sign that there is no fear of God in that person's life. The person who does not fear God, does not realize at those moments of ungodly behavior, he must give in account for his actions at the judgment seat of Christ whether it's in word or deeds according to second Corinthians 5:10.

God had "so" blessed Nehemiah and had given him favor not only of Himself but other humans like the king, that Nehemiah did not have to take a salary or depend on anyone else but God for his sustenance. Be thus reminded that it would have been rightful/lawful if Nehemiah had taken a salary since others before him had, but he chose not to receive a salary. God was his all sufficiency even before he became governor.

Nehemiah could have chosen to do otherwise but his unselfish acts of love and giving showed us why I believe God blessed him in the beginning. It seems to me that in essence Nehemiah was saying, "all that God gives and blessed me with, I will put it all in the work of the Lord." What a great place to be in and what a great testimony that this was to the glory of God!

Verse 16 shows us once again the heart of God's servant, Nehemiah. Not only did he not receive a salary but neither did he lord his position as governor over the people. While previous governors were concerned about their welfare, Nehemiah chose to focus on the Lord's work. He and his servants continued to work on the walls of Jerusalem even without receiving a salary.

A lesser man would not be able to commit himself in this way. He nor his servants tried to take advantage of his poorer brethren by buying up their lands so as to be great land-owners. Nehemiah was guided by principles of service rather than by financial opportunities.

In verses 17-18, Nehemiah gives an accurate account of those who ate at his table. In explaining what was prepared for his table, he was telling what he spent out of his personal funds (since he did not receive a salary as governor) to provide meals for his staff and guests. It appears that he did this for at least 12 years!

A governor or a high-ranking official was expected to entertain lavishly. When Solomon, the third king of Israel dedicated the temple, I Kings 8:62-65, he sacrificed 22,000 cattle and 120,000 sheep and goats, and held a great festival for the assembly for 14 days. This is an indication of what was socially expected for those in high-ranking official positions.

In the case of Nehemiah, each day one ox was slain for food, six choice sheep and some poultry were prepared for the governor's table. He also states that every ten days an abundant supply of all sorts of wine was made available to him, the officials and his guests. Nehemiah paid for the meals prepared for his table. He used what God had already blessed him with. The wealth, possessions, resources and the goods he had, he used them in the services of God. He paid for it because he had it in his possession to pay!

God could get the wealth through Nehemiah for His purposes; therefore, He could get it to him! Nehemiah knew that the hosepipe (him) that was used for watering (blessing the people), got wet too! I believe that when you are a blessing, God will continue to make you a blessing. This man was focused on pleasing God. He had given himself to God, he belonged to God, therefore the possessions, resources, gifts and talents that he had belonged to God as well.

Listen believer, that money you have its God's. The scriptures teach us in Psalms 24:1-2, "The earth is the Lord's and the fulness thereof; the world, and they that dwell therein", verse two," For He hath founded it upon the seas, and established it upon the floods." Also in Psalms 50:10-12, "For every beast of the forest is mine, and the cattle upon a thousand hills", verse 11, "I know all the fowls of the mountain, and the wild beast of the field are mine", verse 12, "If I were hungry, I would not tell thee; for the world is mine and the fullness thereof."

Everything belongs to God. How dare any of us keep that portion of what God has required out of us for His work! Don't talk about that you are serving God, that you love Him, that you are focused but won't use the money and resources that He gives you in His work. That which is in our possession, we are to be a steward over it. We are to manage it for the Lord and His purposes.

When we are focused on the Lord, everything we possess should be used for the glory of God. That voice you have to sing belongs to God's work. How dare you want someone to beg you to use it in the work of God! Those communicating skills, business skills, talents, mercy, love and serving abilities, and helping anointings, all belong to God. Once again, how dare us to hold it from the Lord's work! What we do have, God gave it to us for his pleasure and glory.

When you are focused like Nehemiah and like Mary, (Martha and Lazarus's sister), you don't mind giving your very best for Him. Like Nehemiah who used his wealth in the service of the Lord, Mary gave her Alabaster box. Some say in her box of spices, it contained at least a year's salary of saving. She poured it all on His feet as an honor to Him and an acknowledgment of her love of who Jesus was to her.

Never mind those who tell you to hold on to everything you got. Or those who tell you to spend to satisfy yourself to the neglect of God's work. There are those among us who will not bring the tithes to the work of God often making excuses of saying that was an Old Testament principle. If the patriarchs of old gave tithes under an old covenant, how much more should we tithe and even give more under a new and better covenant?!

When Mary broke her alabaster box and poured the contents on the feet of Jesus, He did not rebuke the disciples for joining in with Judas against Mary for their supposedly concern for the poor. No, what Jesus knew was that they were missing an opportunity to worship with Mary while she gave her best. Here was an opportunity for them to offer their best but they were too blinded, too selfish and too stingy to do so.

We must not be like the rich young ruler in Matthew 19:16-23, who wanted in on the Lord's salvation. He seemingly was sincere in his pursuit of righteousness as he had kept the six commandments Jesus had given him. The rich ruler asked what he lacked? When Jesus told him to sell what he had and give to the poor then come and follow Him, he went away sorrowful for he had great possessions.

At first thought, it seems the young ruler was willing to give himself to Jesus and follow Him. But, after hearing Jesus's last command, he didn't want salvation if it meant giving his possessions also when he comes to Jesus. The above text says he "had great possessions" but really; great possessions had him. God doesn't mind us having things, but He does not want things having and holding us. This seems to be the case more often than not with many of those in the body of Christ. Things God has given us for His glory, now possess us so much so that we can't or won't use them for the glory of God.

There have been many who lost focus and their anointing because they would not obey the Lord when He required something out of them. That "something" that He required, was "something" that He had already given for His services, His glory and His work.

Are you using the possessions He's given you, whether it be wealth, gifts, talents, abilities and skills for His glory? If you are not; why not? It is a bible principle that what you hold on to, what you keep for selfish purposes, you will lose it. The principle also includes the fact that what you give to God's work, you will gain in return in multiple ways!

Nehemiah unselfishly used the resources that God had already given him to bless the work that God called him to do. In verse 19, Nehemiah said to God, "Think upon me, my God, for good according to all I have done for these people." Some may think he was boasting or "tooting his own horn" but I don't think he was doing that. I believe that he was re-minding God of what God has said. I believe Nehemiah was in essence saying, "God remember my good deeds to always be before your mind."

God does tell us in His word (Isaiah 43:26) to put Him in remembrance. In the Bible, even Abraham, Jacob, and Mo-ses, put God in remembrance of His promises to them. We confess God's word, and we can always go to Him and say, "Your word says......in doing so, we are encouraged, and our faith is strengthened. We have revelation from the scripture found in Hebrews 6:10, "For God is not unrighteous to forget your work and labor of love, which you have shown toward His name, in that you have ministered to the saints, and do minister."

When God owns you and He does if you are saved, you have been bought with a price. That price is the precious blood of Jesus, the Christ. Therefore, you shouldn't tell Him that there are certain things you will give Him and others you won't because you want to keep them for yourself. You don't tell Him you are keeping your "alabaster box" for yourself.

When we sacrificially and unselfishly give of whatever that which God has blessed us with, we will be called blessed! The focused Nehemiah not only gave himself to God, but he also gave his possessions willingly and unselfishly. One thing we should note here is that even though he gave on the level he did with his resources; he was never without resources! Praise God.

When the heart is right and your focus is on the Lord, you will freely give of whatever God has graced you with. On the other hand, there are some things God is not going to make you do. He is not going to make you pray spending quality time with Him, fast, obeying Him, giving sacrificially, or even going that extra mile.

I must say it would be to our detriment if we don't do these things just mentioned. But, when you do the fore-mentioned things, God sees it and He rewards it. Deep calleth to deep so says the scriptures. There is a place in God where His eagle believers soar. This journey is not by chance but by choice. When you choose to go deep with God, He will meet you there.

According to Matthew 6:33, If you seek the kingdom of God and His righteousness, all the believers' needs will be met by God's resources. When God knows He can trust you, He will keep on giving you more so you can put those resources into the work of God and Yet... you will have some to spare. If you take care of God's business, He will take care of yours. If you don't use what you have for Him, why do we think God will give us more to consume it upon ourselves to the neglect of building His Kingdom?

If you are wondering, "what if I give my all to God and His work, what then?" I believe you will find that answer in the conversation that Jesus had with Peter in Luke 18 after Jesus had dealt with the rich young ruler telling his disciples that it would be hard for a rich man to enter the Kingdom of God.

Peter said to Jesus in verse 28, "Lo we have left all and followed thee." Jesus replied to Peter's statement of what would happen if he (we) gives our all to follow the Lord. Jesus answers back in verses 29 and 30. "And He said unto them, (not just Peter) Verily I say unto you, there is no man that that left house, or parents, or brethren, or wife, or children, for the Kingdom of God's sake, Who shall not receive manifold more in this present time, and in the world to come life everlasting."

There it is, there is your answer to giving to God and His work. Giving God your substances, your possessions and yourself will always be met by God with more than what you give. I'm reminded of a line in an old song we sang in church at offering time, "You can't beat God's giving no matter how hard you try."

In Luke 6:38, it says give and it shall be given to you, good measure, shaken together, running over shall men give in your bosom. God wants and deserves that we give our best to Him and His works. He gave His best for us when He gave His life on Calvary for the sins of the world. Glory to God in the highest!

Chapter 7

STAY ON THE WALL

The text sets us over into the midst of a plot to overthrow God's servant, Nehemiah. Nehemiah had heard God's voice in going back to Jerusalem to rebuild the burned city and its walls and gates. The first fourteen verses of this chapter deal with opposition through compromise, opposition through slander and through treachery. In every act of aggression against Nehemiah and Israel, these enemies of focus were soundly defeated.

In chapter two, the enemies came against Nehemiah and Israel through scorn and laughter but were defeated. In chapter four, the enemies mocked Nehemiah and the Jews and conspired to fight against Jerusalem and caused Israel to be afraid. The enemy was defeated in his efforts. Further in chapter five, the enemies got among the Jews to turn on one another in covetousness and greed. This scheme too was dismantled and brought to naught.

This chapter helps us to learn more about the devil and his modes of operations as he is up to his old tricks again. One thing we know for sure is that Satan will use people to do his biddings. Once these individuals are employed by the enemy, they recruit others to help them carry out the directions of the devil. We also know that Satan is methodical, if he can't conquer you with one method, he will use another.

We also realize that our common enemy is persistent. Satan works overtime as long as an individual is doing God's will and is reclaiming places that the enemy had his claims on, there will be war. The enemy does not give up easily. The fight is to "death do us apart." The battle will get stronger and stronger with multiple methods. This chapter shows Satan using a different method; more subtle, more conniving, and deceptive. The text will also show that the enemy's schemes will be exposed and brought to naught. The war against Satan will get stronger and stronger, however; if you stand and not give in to the enemy, you will get stronger and stronger!

We further learn that when the devil was defeated in the previous texts, he regrouped almost immediately to launch another attack. When Jesus dealt with the devil in His wilderness encounter in Luke 4:13, Jesus taught us that the devil may leave you after a defeat, but he only leaves for a season. We must be on the alert and not ignorant of Satan's devices.

God had given a vision, a work that He wanted completed and as long as Nehemiah was sensitive, discerning and obedient, God would not let him be defeated by the enemies he would face. Satan wanted Nehemiah to abort what God had already told him. Nehemiah was affected by every act of aggression against him to some degree, however; it did not cause him to cease to do the work assigned to him.

Satan left Nehemiah and Israel for a season, verse 1, "now it came to pass" but right here in the beginning of this chapter, Satan will use these terroristic triplets (Sanballat, Tobiah and Geshem) as well as others once again. The enemies of focus are always looking at whatever progress you are making for the Lord. The news of Nehemiah's progress and work on the wall with no breach (no holes - no breakage) was revealed. The wall was completed but the doors to the gates were not set in place.

Satan, through his embassies, shows up to further halt or stop the work that is being done for God's glory. I like to think another reason that the "triplets" were so inflamed to do harm against the building of the walls is found in Chapter 2:20. Nehemiah reminded the opponents that "ye have no portion, nor right, nor memorial in Jerusalem." The enemies were not allowed to participate in the work of the Lord, this made them angry and jealous.

In verse two, Sanballat and Geshem, sent word to Nehemiah and invited him to a meeting to discuss what he was doing. The enemies wanted to meet in some private place (if you will). They wanted to meet in one of the villages of the plains of Ono. It may have been seen as neutral territory. Nehemiah said "O No" to their invitation! He was saying "you're not going to put me in bondage or trap me."

Their real aim was to stop the work Nehemiah was doing, while pretending that they wanted to work out some agreement with him concerning his work. Nehemiah discerned that their invitation was to do him harm or mischief. Nehemiah was neither stupid nor ignorant of the devil's devices. This servant was not going to let his enemies triple or double team him.

Focused Nehemiah said, in verse 3, (by the way, something that I really liked) to the messenger of Sanballat and Geshem, "I am doing a great work, so that I cannot come down:" He refused to be distracted by these matters and stop what he was doing to get involved with something that he knew would not profit him. Nehemiah further adds, "why should the work cease, whilst I leave it and come down to you?" The answer to his rhetorical question was, "I shouldn't come down" and he didn't! He would not divert his energy from rebuilding Jerusalem's walls. Nehemiah did not allow the distractions to distract him, rather he maintained his focus.

Know this, when you "come up" to do a work for God, there will be those who want you to "come down" from the work of God. Nehemiah recognized the enemy's purpose and would not allow them to get him off course where the vision of God would be put on hold. He would not be thrown off course. He would not allow himself to be put in the hands of these mischievous men that meant him harm.

Even though Nehemiah refused the invitation of his enemies, this defeat did not stop their efforts to thwart the work on the wall. Verse four shows us how persistence the enemies of focus are. They tried to "wear" Nehemiah down by sending him at least four invitations like the first one sent. They sent the same kinds of invitations to meet with him and Nehemiah gave them the same answer as he did at first.

The devil always wants God's people to compromise on what God has given to us. The enemy seeks to scheme us into rebellion against God through our compromise with him. If we compromise, mischief and harm will come to us. Know that as you continue to progress in the work of the Lord, the enemy will try to "wear" you and I down like he did with Nehemiah. We must stand firm and strong and don't come down off the wall.

As stated earlier, when the enemy's tactics don't work at first, he will try another method. On the fifth communication effort to Nehemiah, verse five, the new tactic was in the form of an unsealed letter sent to him by an aide of Sanballat. Apparently, Sanballat wanted the contents of his letter to be known publicly, possibly to invoke fear among the people.

This opposition to the servant of God came in the form of slander. Sanballat began to tell lies against Nehemiah in his letter. It is interesting to me as a leader of a local assembly, that all of Satan's action through the terrible terroristic triplets and others, was directed singularly at Nehemiah. I surmise, if the enemy can get the leader to fall, then it would not be so difficult to defeat the followers.

The content of the letter, in verse six stated, "It was reported among the heathen, and Gashmu saith it, that thou and the Jews think to rebel; for which cause thou buildest the wall, that thou mayest be their king, according to these words." The enemies accused Nehemiah of building the walls so that he could become the king over Jerusalem.

The contents further states in verse seven, that Nehemiah had appointed prophets to make proclamations about the good that was found in him saying, there is a king in Judah. The letter's pressure from Sanballat expressed against Nehemiah was that if he did not meet with him and to have counsel with him, he would tell the king of Persia that he (Nehemiah) was trying to become the new king.

Sanballat admitted that if Nehemiah would not counsel with him, he would tell these lies to the Persian King. The kings of Persia did not tolerate the claims of those who sought their kingship. What was written in the letter was slanderous; it was lies.

Nehemiah replied, through a messenger, regarding the contents of the letter in verse eight. Nehemiah denied the lies and told Sanballat that he had lied to him and furthermore, ALL that he had stated in his letter were lies and that they were formulated in his evil and mischievous heart. Through his experiences with Sanballat, Nehemiah had discerned what Sanballat was trying to do with these lies.

Sanballat wanted to put fear in Nehemiah and the Jewish people so that their hands would be weakened and the work on the wall would stop. The devil will use any tactic at his disposal to get the believer to "come off the wall" but you and I must not come down. We are doing a great work!

Don't be surprised when people used by the devil lie on you. And that their slanderous words will be hurled at you to knock you off the wall. Don't be surprised when accusations from the accuser assaults your character to discredit you and your work for the Lord. This is all the plans of the devil to steal, kill and to destroy, John 10:10. The level of opposition that comes against any of God's servants may be an indication of how great the work is that you are doing! So, stay on the wall, don't come down! If you are not focused, get focused. If your focus is dimmed, re-focus or maintain your focus on the assignment that God has given you!

The letter from Sanballat, even though it contained lies, had an effect on Nehemiah and the Jewish people. He says in verse nine as he prays to God to strengthen his hands, that the letter did cause some fear among them. That the fear would cause their hands to be so weak, that the work would not be done.

Even though I'm sure Nehemiah had Israel in mind asking God to help their hands as well, but he needed the strength from God to stand. He knew he could not allow fear to creep in his life and paralyze him from the work. Nehemiah wanted to maintain his focus. Satan's intent today is to get you over into fear. Satan knows and we should know, when you are in fear, you are out of faith.

Let's not allow the enemy to remove us from our faith posture by getting in agreement with his lies. Don't be surprised when Satan tries to get you to change what God has said so you would believe a lie. God had said build, but Satan says bow to his agenda. When Satan speaks, he lies because he is the father of lies.

Satan's lies seek to attack the word of God on three levels. He attacks the authority of God's word. Secondarily he attacks the accuracy of the word of God and thirdly he attacks the acceptability of God's word. These three prongs can all be found in Genesis 3:1-8 when Satan was dealing with Eve in the garden of Eden.

We live by faith and not by sight. Those that have been justified by God, walk by faith. Faith is so important that the scriptures say, without faith it is impossible to please God. When we allow fear to control our lives, we are in the flesh and those in the flesh cannot please God. Fear seeks to chase faith right out of our lives.

The devil's mode of operation is virtually the same. If he can't stop you on his first offensive attack, he will continue with other methods and tactics. Satan had used Sanballat, Tobiah, Geshem and others, but had been unsuccessful in stopping Nehemiah and his Jewish brethren from the vision God had given them.

Here in the text of verses 10-13, a false prophet had been hired to put Nehemiah in fear of his life and to compromise his faith stance. Nehemiah had gone into the community and visited the home of a fellow Jew. This Jew, Shemaiah, was shut up in his house, may be directed by the three terrorists to pretend that he was in fear for his life so that Nehemiah might fear as well. The false prophet told Nehemiah that they should go to the house of the Lord (go inside the temple, shut the doors) and if he didn't go there, he would be killed that night. Nehemiah stood boldly in faith with a discerning spirit, responded to the directive of Shemaiah and told him that he was not going to follow his suggestion. Nehemiah insisted that a man of his caliber was not going to run and hide from his enemies. Nehemiah knew who he was and who he belonged to.

He also knew God was protecting him and that the "word" given to him by this "for hire prophet" Shemaiah, was not sent by God but rather sent/hired by the triplets! Nehemiah realized that if he had given in to the false prophet he would have sinned before God and his reputation as a man of God would be in question and his leadership would be discredited.

The man of God chose to take this matter to God in prayer once again, verse 14, he knows that the battle is the

Lords'. Nehemiah made this opposition a spiritual warfare rather than fighting in his flesh to defeat his enemies. An old song we sang in our church had a line in it that says, "If I hold my peace and let the Lord fight my battles, victory shall be mine." Nehemiah asks God to remember what Tobiah and Sandballat, the prophetess, Noadiah, and other prophets had done to intimidate him.

Just know that being a Christian and obeying what God wants you to do is not always easy! There will be challenges but stay focused. Keep praying, don't let the devil throw us off course with your assignment from God. We must "stay on the wall" and not come down. It is not the will of God for the devil to hinder, stop or overthrow the work of the Lord.

If the work is truly of God, the only way for the devil to overthrow it is for those laborers He has chosen to do the work, allow, permit or give authority to the devil to stop the work. The scriptures teach us in I Peter 5:8, "Be sober, be vigilant; because your adversary the devil, as a roaring lion, walketh about, seeking whom he MAY devour." The devil must have your permission to destroy you or your assignment. It's not a matter of his ability because he CAN destroy. But oftentimes we give him (the devil) permission through our ignorance, and he takes full advantage of that permission. The work will be stopped or haltered when the worker gives the devil permission. The work will be stopped or hindered when we fight in the FLESH which will get you over into disobedience. Romans 6:8 says, "So then they that are of the flesh cannot please God." The work will fail when the workers get into FEAR and out of FAITH. The scriptures in Romans 14:23c teach us, "that which is not of faith is sin."

God heard the focused and righteous prayer of Nehemiah, verse 15, and the work of the Lord was completed in record time. The walls and gates were rebuilt in fifty-two days! When the enemies of the work, verse 16, saw what God had done through Nehemiah and the Jews, "they were much cast down in their own eyes; for they perceived that his work was wrought of our God."

It has been a repeated refrain when it comes to the devil's efforts to stop the saints in their efforts to please the Lord in the work He has given us to complete. After every defeat suffered by the devil, he will always re-group with another strategy to continue his opposition. Here in verses 17-19, the believer must be careful because many that you think should be supporters of the work of God are traitors!

Some of the nobles of Judah exchanged letters with Tobiah and were sold out in support of him. You do recall that this man Tobiah was one third of the terroristic terrible triplets who constantly harassed and tried to humiliate Nehemiah and the work he was doing for the Lord? Many of these Jews had sworn unto him because of an influential family relationship he had in Judah. Tobiah's son Jehohanan was married to the daughter of Meshullam, who had helped repair the wall of Jerusalem. These traitors, who needed to refocus, reported to Nehemiah the good deeds they thought Tobiah did.

Nehemiah responded with his own words back to them and they forwarded his communication to Tobiah. I believe Nehemiah told Tobiah the same message he had given earlier in Chapter 2:20, where he says, "you have no portion, nor right, nor memorial in Jerusalem." Nehemiah was saying you are not part of this work. You are not part of this vision. Upon receiving the messages that Nehemiah sent, Tobiah sent additional letters to the man of God to put him in fear.

The text does not tell us the content of the letters, but you can rest assured it was more of the same things he had said previously. These last few verses alert us to the fact that while you are in this spiritual warfare doing a work for the Lord, you must remain vigilant against your known opponent, the devil. Nothing is beyond his evil imagination to fight against you. Even when it seems like we have completed and jumped over one hurdle, one loop, and one obstacle, there is no time to relax because the devil is still busy trying to steal, kill and to destroy you.

Like Nehemiah you are doing a great work and you can't come down off the wall. No matter the opposition, the humiliation, the ridicule, the mockery and fear, stay on the wall (the work of the Lord) and complete the Lord's assignment for your life. Satan won't give up easily, the fight is till death do us part. The battle will get stronger and stronger, but if you stand you will get stronger and stronger, and you will see the salvation of the Lord. The Lord will build the walls and close the breach, set the gates and doors in place in supernatural timing.

Chapter 8

ORDER IN THE HOUSE

As we continue to explore this powerful book of Nehemiah, we come to this chapter and find a chapter that is full of words/names that are hard to pronounce! At first glance one might look at the names and go on to the next chapter as far as preaching/teaching is concerned; however, I do think there are some things in the chapter that one could pull out that are of some worth and of value.

The walls have been built in a record time of 52 days despite the opposition and distractions that the Israelites faced. The heathens and the enemies recognized that the hand of the Lord had caused the work to be completed. Yet, there were those in Israel who had worked on the wall and were still trying to get Nehemiah to accept Tobiah; a member of the terrible triplets who continually harassed Nehemiah. Tobiah had gained support from some of the Jews. These Jews had lost their focus on the things of God and really needed to refocus on the Lord's work. Nehemiah knew and told Tobiah that he and the enemies of the Lord had no part in what God was doing and did do. Tobiah wrote letters to Nehemiah to put him in fear. Still, Nehemiah overcame yet more opposition in various forms from those who would stop the work of the Lord.

In chapter seven, verse one, the walls were built, the doors set up and then Nehemiah began to organize the people of Israel so that he could see who all that would make up the body of Israel. Nehemiah was setting the house of Israel

66

in order. Nehemiah recognized it would not do much good to have the physical structure of the wall completed and in order if there was no order and organization behind the walls!

This chapter may be explained in four different divisions. These divisions are Delegation of the People, Designation of the People, Denial of privileges to certain People and Dispense of Resources from some of the People.

Delegation (Appointing) of the People

Nehemiah began to appoint porters (gate keepers) even though the walls were built. Nehemiah had discernment to know that the enemies of Israel would still try to hinder and stop the work, break through the walls and to cause damage to it. This is probably one of the reasons that he continued to reject the recommendation of Tobiah to him by some of the Israelites. He realized the trouble and opposition that Tobiah had presented to him earlier.

Nehemiah also appointed singers. This is interesting because he recognized the value of praise and worship to God from God's people. As a being created by God, He made us as a praise unto Him. The word of God tells us in Psalms 150, let everything that has breath praise the Lord. Nehemiah also appointed Levites who would conduct the sacrificial services and do work in the temple.

In verse two, Nehemiah continues to delegate authority so as to keep order among the Israelites. Even though Nehemiah was the visionary/leader and governor, he realized that it took more than one person to complete the work of the Lord. Nehemiah had been the governor of Jerusalem and was probably going to return to the King of Persia where he had served as cupbearer. Now, he gives authority and delegates power to individuals by the name of Hanani and Hananiah. These men had a great reputation with God and Nehemiah, they were faithful and feared God above many others. These men had rulership of the palace and command of the fortress. God can and will use faithful individuals to continue His work as one faithful leader leaves the scene.

As the leader delegates authority, he must also give instructions on how to move forward. It would be unprofitable to appoint someone to a position(s) and that person had no direction on how to proceed and maintain order among the people. Nehemiah gave instructions in verse 3 for the newly delegated leaders.

The instructions included that even while the watchmen were still on guard, the doors were to be shut and barred. The gates of the city of Jerusalem would not be opened until the sun was hot. Normally the gates would be opened at dawn, but the gates' opening was to be delayed until the sun was high in the heavens to prevent the enemy from making a surprise attack before most of the people were up from their nights' sleep. Residential guards were to be appointed from Jerusalem to protect the walls as well as the homes in the area. Verse four tells us that the city was large but sparsely populated with few people in it. Their homes had not yet been rebuilt. While delegation is of utmost importance, instructions for that delegated place is important as well.

Designating of the People

Nehemiah said, in verse five, that God had given him a plan to organize Israel so as to see who really was a part of the tribes of Israel, and to see what resources they had available to use in bringing Israel in line with God's covenant for them. Nehemiah assembled the nobles, the officials and the common people for a registration by families. The people were to be designated by their family lineage.

Nehemiah had found the genealogical record of those who had been the first to return to Jerusalem. The group of people and their descendants were those who had been in

Babylonian captivity and had returned to Jerusalem. The Babylonian King Nebuchadnezzar had invaded Jerusalem and had taken captives, and many had now returned to their beloved city and providence under the leadership of several leaders.

We must understand that after the Babylonian captivity, Zerubbabel had led a group back to Jerusalem 94 years before Nehemiah. Ezra (the scribe) had led a group back to Jerusalem 13 years before Nehemiah. Of these three expeditions, there were remnants/leaders of families who were still there at various ages. Verse seven gives us the names of some of these leaders.

From verses eight to 63, there is a list of the names of various people who would make up the core of Israel in Jerusalem. The list of names includes the number of each family tribe. Read the names as you please, good luck with your pronunciation of the names! All these named people had to have a pedigree (a blood heritage) if they would be part of this organization of the Jewish family of Israel. In this list of people, it included the men of Israel, the priests, the Levites, the servants (temple assistants) including Solomon's servants.

For us as members and believers in His church today, we are required to have the right bloodline to be a part of this special order called the "Body of Christ." We share in the precious blood of Jesus Christ. When we accept Jesus as our savior, we become a part of the greatest family (the church/ the body of Christ) upon the face of the earth. This makes us a designated and prepared people by being bought and redeemed with the precious blood of Jesus as He shed His blood on that cruel Roman cross of execution. We then become family members because of our blood heritage in Jesus Christ. Our destination is in Him in heavenly places. We have royal blood connection with God through

Jesus Christ our Lord and Savior. We've been made to sit together with Him in heavenly places far above principalities and powers! What a lofty place that has been designated for us by virtue of us accepting Jesus Christ as Lord of our lives.

Denying privileges for some of the People

From verses 61 to 63, we find some people who were denied the privilege of being a part of the makeup of the organization of Israel. It is interesting that this list of people had come up from Persian cities. They had worked on the wall; they had helped Nehemiah and Israel rebuild and refurbish the walls and gates. But when it came time to include them in the organizing of Israel-they were not able as they could not show their lineage to Israel. These people included the children of Delilah (one of her sons was Shemaiah, who had been shut up in the temple and wanted Nehemiah to hide with him in the temple, chapter 6:10), the other sons were Tobiah and Nekoda. The total number of these people was 642 persons.

Included also in the list of those persons who were denied the privilege to serve were priests as described in verse 63. Various names were listed who claimed priesthood. In searching the genealogy, their names were not found, therefore they were denied the privilege to serve as priests. The listed men were considered polluted and not appointed nor anointed to serve in the capacity as priest. In verse 65, the Tirshatha (another name for the governor, Nehemiah) denied the unregistered priests to participate in the roles of priests.

The priests had the responsibility to minister about the holy things of God. These men were also denied the privilege to eat of the most holy things of God until further examination and instruction from God be done through the Urim and Thummim. The Urim and Thummim was a device used by God for the people of God to get His counsel on various concerns. During this dispensation when the Urim and Thummim was used, the holy spirit was not living inside of the people as the holy spirit had not been given at large to the people at this time. The spirit of God had come upon various individuals to do a certain work for God, but the holy spirit did not dwell in the people like He does now in the New Testament dispensation which we now live in.

In verses 66-67, it gives the number of people who were found in the genealogy and that number was 42,360 citizens. Also, included with the number were slaves, servants and singers both men and women to be added to the total count. Verses 68-69 gives an account of the resources that were found among the people.

Today, to be included in the body of Christ a person must be born again. An individual must allow Jesus through the holy spirit to come into their lives as they repent and ask Him to live inside of them. People may join a church but that does not mean that they are a part of Jesus's body. Only those who have believed in Jesus to the saving of their souls are part of His body. Those who are saved have privileges that others outside of the body of Christ do not have. The saved will not be denied any of the promises of God as we use our faith to receive what He has promised us.

Dispensing of Resources by some of the People

It is a spiritual principle that God blesses His people so that in turn we may be a blessing to others. Everything God blesses you and I with is not just for us! God wants us to share with others who are less fortunate than we are, and He wants us to give toward His causes. We are reminded in the scriptures that according to Deuteronomy 8:18, where it says; "But thou shalt remember the Lord thy God: for it is he that giveth thee power to get wealth, that he may establish his covenant which he sware unto thy fathers, as it is this day." What we gain financially really comes from God as He empowers and prospers us to obtain. We are then responsible to give as He instructs us to give. He wants to establish His covenant (His will and desires) for the earth and His people.

From verses 70-72, it gives a list of the various individuals who gave toward the work of the Lord. The scriptures identify who these individuals were. The first group of people who gave were "some" of the chiefs of the fathers who gave to the treasure so that their resources would be available to continue the work of the Lord. The amount and what this group gave is listed. They gave gold and silver. Notice the scripture said it was "some" of the fathers that gave. It suggests to me that all could have given but only "some" gave. This is true in our local assemblies as well. Some give liberty, some give sparingly, and some do not give at all.

In the New Testament a couple pretended to give on a level commensurate to what might be expected of those in leadership positions. Ananias and Saphiria were exposed as those not being honest and they severely paid a price for their dishonest actions. The couple "dropped dead" before the congregation that they were trying to impress. Their bodies had to be carried away to their burial ground. Leaders in every local church ought to be an example when it comes to giving and not withholding their resources that could advance the kingdom of God. Robbing God when He has given you necessary resources could result in disastrous consequences as did the above-named couple.

A need or a concern can be presented to the local body of Christ and yet everyone won't respond in giving. No matter what your financial portfolio is, everyone can give something. Your giving may not be as much as someone else, but you still can give in principle on (how you prospered) toward the work of the Lord. A real servant knows he or she does not have to compete with another believer when it comes to how much you give. The real servant realizes that he gives in proportion as God has blessed him. However, the servant doesn't shut out the voice of God as He speaks to him regarding giving to His work.

Verse 70 also tells us that the Tirshatha (another name for the governor) which at the time was Nehemiah gives to the work of the Lord. You recall that Nehemiah took no salary as the governor, yet he was able to care and provide for his entire staff on a daily basis! Nehemiah was able to provide for his staff because God had provided for him. And now, we still see the man of God giving yet more. God found in Nehemiah a man He could trust with wealth. Nehemiah was willing to give to the cause of God without hesitation. When God finds (surprise, He already knows) a person that He can trust with great resources, He will continue to make sure that person has something to give as well as being able to provide for his own needs without lack! Remember when a hosepipe waters the ground, the hosepipe gets wet as well! When we sow bountifully, God will make sure we will stay "wet" with His (water) resources! What a mighty God we serve!

The scriptures identify another group who gave to the work other than leaders and Nehemiah who gave. The scripture simply describes them as "the rest of the people." Distributing your resources as God has prospered you is not just for the leadership but the "laymen" as well. The "lay" membership (those who are not necessarily in leadership positions) gave in kind as did the leaders, they gave gold and silver as well as some priestly garments for the priest who ministered before the Lord.

Verse 73 begins with the word "So" which I believe is indicative of what has just transpired. The various ones listed above had given and it made it possible for the priest, the Levites, the porters and singers who had no homes of their own to reside in a home. This aforementioned group usually owned no homes as they now would be provided one because of faithful giving by those who heard God on the stewardship of giving. Because of the tremendous outpouring of giving that took place, the people were able to be established in their homes in their various cities. The corporate body of any local church would never suffer any lack if all the people would give on the level that God has prospered them. Dispensing the resources that God has put in our hands is important if the work of God here on earth would be successful. As the order of delegation, designation and even denial of certain privilege takes place in the church's order; know that dispensing (giving) to the Lord's work is also very much in order.

Chapter 9

RE-FOCUSING ON THE WORD OF THE LORD

In the previous chapter, Nehemiah had "set the house in order." He delegates (appoints and instructs) designates, denies and dispenses resources. These acts of Nehemiah were to position Israel spiritually so that God could bless them as they could and would renew their covenant with Him. Nehemiah knew the importance of order. He knew chaos would result among the people if there was no order among them. Israel would have remained in the deplorable and declining condition that he found them in when he came to Jerusalem if there would be no order among them. If the people of God needed to be put in order, then it would be the word of the Lord that would help them maintain that order.

During the Babylonian captivity there was no mention of public worship or reading of the word of the Lord among the Israelites who had once adhered to it. For any organization to stay in order, (here, the people of God) there needs to be some guidelines to ensure its continued order, effectiveness and longevity. This chapter invites the returned exiles to re-focus on the Word of the Lord that had been lost or abandoned by the very people it was written to and written for. This Word of the Lord would guide them in His ways and wisdom.

From verse one, we learned that Ezra the "ready" scribe had now joined with Nehemiah in Jerusalem. Ezra had in his possession the Word of the Lord that had been given to Moses by the hand of God as commandments to the Israelites. Ezra, Nehemiah and other leaders would have Israel to refocus on the Word of the Lord. Verse four gives the names of others who would encourage and cause the people to refocus and to understand and to follow the book of the Law of Moses.

It is interesting to note that ALL the people came out as one man in the streets before the water gate. All the word of God is for all of God's people. If you would be a follower of God, you can't pick and choose which part of the word you will follow because it goes against your fleshly desires. The only possible exceptions are when the word speaks specifically to the Jews and not to those of us who have been grafted into covenant with God through the new birth under the New Testament dispensation. There are some words given to Israel that do not apply to New Testament believers, like some dietary laws and sacrificing animals for atonement. Jesus is our once and for all sacrifice as the lamb of God slain from the foundation of the world. (Revelation 13:8).

You may recall in Chapter 3 where it talks about the Watergate. The Water gate (chapter 3:26-27) may speak of the word of God which cleans the believer. The Israelites positioned themselves at the water gate and it was a bold statement that the people wanted to hear the word of God so they would continue to be cleansed. The scripture says we are cleansed by the washing of the word of God.

The united people asked Ezra to bring the word of the Lord out to them and read it as it had been given to Moses. People who are in the process of repenting or have repented and have seen the error of their ways know that if they would continue to please God, they needed His instructions and His commandments. In Israel's history they were known to drift from God when they would lose focus on the Word of the

Lord. So, now they asked that the Word of the Lord be read to them so they could comply and continue in the order that had been established for them.

As requested, verse two, Ezra brought the book of the Law out upon the first day of the seventh month to the people both men and women and to those who could understand what was being read to them. Perhaps this part of the scripture may have been written because it said All the people came out to hear the reading of the word. The audience may have and most likely included children and those born in exile who knew very little if anything regarding the Laws of Moses.

Even if our children don't understand the Word of the Lord when they hear it, nevertheless they should be in attendance where the Word is being taught or preached. It becomes the responsibility of the parents/caregivers to further explain and communicate the Word of God to our children on a level that they can understand the general principles of the Word of the Lord. The scripture teaches us in Proverbs 22:6, "to train up our children in the ways of the Lord (the way he should go) and when they are old, they will not depart." Notice it is not the way the child wants to go, but rather the way he should go, there is a big difference here!

In verse 3, Ezra read the book at the watergated from morning to midnight! So much for today's sermons of a rushed ("you better be through in thirty minutes") presentation so that the people of God can get to their favorite restaurant before a crowd beats them there! The scripture says of this audience, that they were attentive to the Word of the Lord. They were not looking at "their watches" or the sun trying to time how long Ezra could/would read! They weren't passing notes on stone tablets or using their "cell phones" to browse the "internet" for the latest happenings or playing some silly mindless game on their phones while reading and ministry was taking place. They were attentive to the word that was being read/ministered to them in their hearing. Unlike some of today's hearers, they were not trying to find fault with the Word of God and its' presenters; (preachers or teachers) rather they were submitted to the word they heard.

There is a story in the New Testament (Acts 20:9), where when the Apostle Paul was preaching late into the night, (what is called long-winded!) that a young man sitting in a window, named Eutychus who was supposed to be listening to the sermon being preached, fell asleep and he fell to his death. Thank God for mercy and grace because there would be many who have fallen asleep during worship service and the undertakers would have to be called for them!

The hearer should be attentive when the Word of God is being taught or preached, it is that important! A good, seasoned orator will discern when his or her audience has received enough "spiritual feeding" during that particular worship experience. I beg you and it's in your best interest that you don't tune out and certainly don't go to sleep while the word is being presented!

Ezra, in verse four, stood on a pulpit (a raised platform made of wood) a little above the people so he could be seen by the congregation as he read. The emphasis, mind you, was not on Ezra but on the word of God. But, if you stand for the word and with the word, it will make you stand above others who disobey, disrespect or dismiss the word!

On either side of Ezra were capable men who stood with him to interpret the Word written in the Hebrew language into the Armenian language so that the people could understand. These men stood as a testimony to the truth of what Ezra was saying. They stood with the man of God as he shared the Word of the Lord. It is imperative that the man or woman of God in our local assemblies have support especially of the leaders in that congregation when it comes to teaching and preaching and obeying the Word of the Lord.

In verses five and six, Ezra opened the Book to read it as he stood above the people on the purposeful pulpit. As he stood to read, the people stood up in respect to the Word of the Lord, their focus was now on God's word as it was given to Moses. Ezra blessed the great God, and all the people said Amen, Amen which means "we agree" with you. They lifted their hands in Pentecostal fashion and bowed their heads in humility and respect. They worshiped the Lord with their faces to the ground.

It would be awesome if all the members of our local churches today would focus and honor the word of the Lord like these returned Jews did when Ezra read the Word of the Lord to them. There are many among the body of Christ who seem to want to change what the Word of the Lord says to fit their liberal and compromising position/agendas.

For an example at the writing of this narrative, a fifty-year-old decision that allowed abortion to be legal has been over-turned. I believe it never should have been legally sanctioned in the first place. However, opponents still believe that they should be able to kill these babies as they do not recognize the babies as humans or don't care if they are. It is a shame that even bible touting, church going people have not decided whether abortion in general is wrong. There are possible exceptions with abortion when it comes to the life of the mother or in cases on incest or rape but not as a general means of contraception after a sexual encounter without birth contraceptive and the woman becomes pregnant. God said to Jeremiah that He knew him before he was formed in his mothers' womb. God recognized and knew that Jeremiah was a human being before he was born. To kill (abort, is now a more sophisticated term for murder) these little underdeveloped humans is against the word of the Lord.

Another example comes to mind when thinking about same sex marriages. I know this is a touchy subject for some today, but I believe that the Bible speaks to this subject very clearly. Marriages should be between a male and a female totally committed to each other until death due them apart. Some proponents of the same sex union states that "love is love" meaning as long as you love another person whether romantically or sexually regardless of gender, it is alright with God. I disagree with this philosophy wholeheartedly. What some people are calling love is abnormal, an abomination and animalistic lust which is not the God kind of love that is shared between a committed man and woman under the auspices of God. Thank God for those who rightly divide the Word of God that is consistent and congruent with other passages found in the Word of God. They do not try to take isolated passages to prove an unnatural position in defiance to God's known will for man.

A group of men who were probably all Levites in verse seven, went through the gathered assembly as the people stood still and they helped the people to understand the word that was being read to them. It was important that the congregation know what was being said so they could comply with the Laws of Moses given to him by God. An expected outcome of obedience should accompany their understanding of the Word as it was being explained to them. When one considers what has just transpired in the previous first through seventh verses and now including verse eight, it looks like the perfect church gathering for us today, notice the following:

The people assembled together to hear the word of God. Hebrews 10, says that we should not forsake the assembly of ourselves together, they did this. The word was exalted very highly. In every church assembly the Word of God should take priority. They had respect for the Word as seen when they stood to hear it read. The priest/scribe (for us to-day, the preacher), read and explained the word assisted by others so that the people could understand it. The people wept at the hearing of the word. Among the congregants there was a sincerity in their participation of the events transpiring. Their weeping may be a result of them recognizing their sins and repenting for them. As needed, repentance should take place in all our assemblies. The actions of the congregation of Israel looks like the "perfect" church gathering on any given worship day.

This special holy day was a day of rejoicing. In verse nine, Nehemiah, Ezra and the Levites expressed to the people that what they were experiencing was holy unto the Lord and it should be to them as well. They were instructed not to mourn or weep but rather rejoice. This is indicated in verse 10, when they were told to go their way, eat the fat, drink the sweet, and send portions unto to those who were less fortunate who didn't have the finances to purchase celebratory items. The ministerial crew of Nehemiah, Ezra and the Levites, verse 11, who calmed the people down reiterated the fact that the day was holy and for the congregation and for them not to be sorrowful or grievous, but rather rejoice, for the joy of the Lord was their strength. As the congregation had repented of their sins, it would not be necessary for them to continually be sorrowful.

Whether you know it or not or refuse to believe it, it does not take all day to repent! If you mean business with God when you hear the Word, you repent, and purpose to obey that word, you can wipe away the tears from your eyes. If you have become holy again in practice (from a disobedient place), you can get excited about the word and the work of God again that is wrought in you by your great God. Quit mourning and weeping and start shouting! The moment one truly repents, you can begin to rejoice for your sins have been forgiven and covered by the blood of Jesus, you New Testament believer! Hallelujah and thank God for His amazing grace! The congregation, in verse 12, adhered to the instructions given to them and they went away and made great mirth (great rejoicing) as they understood the words that were declared unto them.

True repentance and true rejoicing do not stop in a day! On the second day, verse 13, the chief/head fathers of houses, the priests and Levites came to Ezra to learn and understand yet more about God's divine will and instructions for them found in the Book of the Law. Here is a great lesson for us New Testament believers, you never learn enough of the word of God where you think you now know enough of it. Real genuine believers continue to seek and knock, hunger and thirst for righteousness because they know that they will be filled, and new doors of understanding will be opened to them.

In their seeking, verse 14, they found where it was written in the Law that the Lord had commanded through Moses from the book of Leviticus that the Israelites should dwell in booths during the Feast of the seventh month, they were in the seventh month. This feast is associated with the Feast of Tabernacles. These booths were "homemade " temporary houses/huts made of branches so that the Jews could dwell in them for at least seven days during the Feast of Tabernacle celebration. To dwell in these booths was a reminder to the people of God to the fact that they were pilgrims leaving Egypt going into Canaan and did not own their homes.

In verse 15, the revelation of celebrating the Feast of Tabernacle was to be published throughout Jerusalem among the Jews. They were to gather palm branches, olive branches, pine branches and myrtle branches and other thick leafy branches from other trees to make booths in accordance with the Laws of Moses. Verse 16-17 reminds us that it's one thing to hear the word with joy, but it's another thing to hear and obey the word given to you. They made booths on the roofs of their houses, in the courts, in the courts of the house of God and in the streets of the city. What a picture of unity among the believing assembly. All the people participated in doing what the Word had instructed them to do. There is a saying that is often said, "when you learn better you do better." This act of worship had been neglected since the days of Joshua which includes their years of captivity in Babylon. But when we hear and obey the Word of the Lord, we will do better and there will be great joy as you and I obey it!

One by-product of obeying the Word of God is this-there was very great gladness. Our churches would benefit by imitating the actions of these former exile Jews who had refocused on the Word of the Lord. There would be more joy and gladness among the people of God instead of gloom and sadness. The psalmist said, "I was glad when they said unto me let us go into the house of the Lord." Instead of being glad when worship time begins, many saints are sad! Day by day, verse 18 indicates, the children of Israel continued to seek God's will and instructions from the book of the law of God.

Just because you receive one revelation from God's word, don't stop your pursuit of God, He has much more to reveal to us. You won't receive everything you need concerning your future and destiny in one reading session or one sermon from an anointed messenger. You must continue in the word of God.

In John 8:31-32, "Then said Jesus to those Jews which believed on him, if ye continue in my word, then you are my disciples indeed, and if ye shall know the truth, and the truth shall make you free." I might add, it's the truth you know and obey that will make you free! Stay in the Word of God no matter the situations or circumstances.

Stay with the Word when you are glad and even when you are sad! The Word works when you work (obey and receive) the Word! The Israelites kept the feast for seven days and on the eighth day, they culminated the Feast of Tabernacle with a closing celebration that was to be done based on the ordinances of God found in the Book of the Laws of Moses.

In concluding this eighth chapter, I want to share with you six points from the chapter.

1. The Word of God is of utmost importance, Nehemiah and Ezra and the Levites showed us its importance. There will be no order, no peace, no faith nor blessings without the word of God. The earth (cosmos/world) was framed by God's words. God's word is immutable; unchanging, without error and contradictions. Is the Word of God the final authority over your life? The word was read for several hours from morning to midday! That's how important the Word was to them, and the people listened attentively.

2. Because the Word is important, there ought to be a Respect for it. A pulpit was built so that the Word could be heard above the crowd. The people stood up in respect for the Word. So, how do you treat the Word of God when it is read, taught or preached in your presence? Are you turned off by it, do you rebel at it, do you fall asleep when its' preached or simply disobey the Word when you hear it? The people in the text lifted their hands, bowed their heads and turned their faces to the ground in awe because the Word of the Lord was being read to them. There ought to be a

healthy respect for the Word of God among all believers.

3. The Word of God will bring about Conviction. In the text, when the Word went forth in a marathon manner, it convinced and convicted the people to confess their sins. This was expressed as they wept and mourned over their sins as the Word brought conviction on them. They saw the error of their way by hearing and heeding the word. When the Word of God goes forth there will be conviction even though one may resist that conviction. The Apostle Peter used the Word of God as he preached on the day of Pentecost and the Word brought about conviction and caused thousands to repent and be saved.

4. The Word of God Cleans. When conviction comes and repentance is done, cleansing will be a by-product of that repentance. The scripture says in I John 1:9, that "if we confess our sins; that is to agree with God regarding the fact that what we are doing is wrong in His eyesight, he is faithful and just to forgive us our sins, and to cleanse us from all unrighteousness." The Word will cleanse you and I from wrong thoughts, words and actions. The Word will establish our thought life and help us take on the mind of Christ so that we can think and speak what He says. Jesus says in John 15:3, "Now ye are clean through the Word which I have spoken to you." Israel got cleansed while receiving the Word of the Lord.

5. The Word of God will Correct. The Word will cause us to do better when you learn better if you have a desire to live for the Lord. Israel found some things in the Law of Moses (the Word of the Lord for them at that time) things that they had neglected and were not doing. God had established some ordinances and com-

mandments for them to follow but they were not obeying them. However, when the people understood what the Word was expecting out of them, they corrected the error of their ways. It ought to be the same with the New Testament Body of Christ today, when we discover our sins and errors, we should correct our fallen ways and come in alignment with what the Word of God commands of us. There is life in the Word of God for He says my Words are life. We ought to want life instead of death! In the kingdom of God, everything that is out of order will be corrected only by the Word of God.

6. Finally, when we repent and obey the Word, there will be rejoicing and gladness! When Israel repented and obeyed God there was rejoicing and gladness. An immediate celebration took place among the adherents to the Word. They celebrated over the Word that they had received. They celebrated even more when they found out about the Feast of Tabernacle. They experienced seven full days of joyous celebration and then concluded with an eighth day holy assembly.

When the people repented and obeyed God, they found out that the "joy of the Lord was their strength." There is an urgent need for the people of God to Refocus our attention back to the Word of the Lord. Let us get back to what is already written and decided upon for us as believers by God and leave our rationalities alone and rediscover what will give us life and peace, that is the Word of God!

Chapter 10

Nehemiah 9:1-38, 10:1-39, 11:1-36, 12:1-26

COVENANTED AND COMMITTED TO WALKING IN THE WORD

This presentation will encompass chapters nine, ten, eleven and part of chapter twelve. The four chapters lend themselves to a continued flow with the contextual content under discussion of the aforementioned title. The chapters taken together will in no wise lose the meaning of the message presented here.

In the last message as you recall, the emphasis was on re-focusing on the Word of God. The Word had been laid aside, neglected, omitted and overlooked. But Israel had found the Book of the Law that was given to Moses, and it was read to the congregation, and they began to put it into practice. The Word of God would be the standard bearer for order among the people. The Word would be the mechanism whereby the nation of Israel would be put in place, put in an order that would please God so that His blessings would come upon His chosen people.

A few practical points were given in the last message and are presented again for the content of the message at hand. The following points should be implemented in our lives as New Testament believers as well.

1. The Word is of utmost importance. Heaven and earth will pass away before the Word does, so says the Bible. God stands over His Word to perform it. He will do what He says.

2. There should be a healthy respect for the Word of God. When the Word of God was read to the people, they stood in respect to it. They lifted their hands and bowed their heads, and they turned their faces to the ground in respect to the Word of God.
3. The Word will bring about conviction even though an individual may shun that conviction. When the Word went forth, they confessed their sins and began to weep and mourn as they were convicted.
4. The Word of God cleanses the believer. Repentance is done after conviction takes place and cleansing is a by-product of that process. The New Testament scripture, I John 1:9, teaches us that, if we confess our sins, God is faithful and just to forgive us and cleans us from all unrighteousness.
5. The Word of God will correct unrighteous behavior. The Word of God will cause us to do better when we know better. The Word of God gives us the proper way to carry out the mandates of God.
6. When respect for the Word of God is honored, and conviction is experienced and cleansing takes place with the individual, rejoicing and gladness will take place! There will be joy and the Word says in Nehemiah 8:10c, "the joy of the Lord is our strength."

In these four chapters under consideration, Nehemiah and Ezra were leading the congregation into further committing themselves in a deeper and more conscious way to walk in the Word that they were now re-focusing upon. In essence they were becoming covenant minded and committed to walking in the Word that they heard. It's one thing to "have" a leather-bound copy of the Bible on your coffee table at home for some form of decoration yet it is another thing for you to "read" the Book. Still, it is another thing to "hear" a sermon preached or a lesson taught from the Bible and yet not "walk" in the Word. Too often this is the case among many hearers of the Word today. Our obedience to God should cause us to walk in the Word of God on a daily basis.

Nehemiah chapters nine, ten, eleven and a part of twelve gives us the opportunity to combine the chapters together and to share this word in an outline form. The outline will begin and use the letter "S" for each point, perhaps for easy memory recall. The following are the points beginning with the letter S: Sanctification, Separation, Servants, Survey, Saints, Stipulation, Selected and Sacred will be the outlined discussed going forward.

Sanctification

The discussion on the Sanctification of Israel in preparation of keeping the Covenant-God's Word is presented here. In chapter nine verse one, on the twenty fourth day of the seventh month, Israel was assembled with fasting, putting on sackcloths and putting earth on their bodies. Fasting was a form of emptying themselves from physical food so that God could fill them spiritually. Sackcloths represented humility. They had recognized and knew within themselves that they were nothing without God. Putting earth "dirt" on themselves was further expressing deep humility and submission to God. Israel realized their origin as they were made from dirt and God breathed into them the breath of life and they became living souls.

They had re-focused on the Word of God and now they were giving themselves totally over to God so that they could carry out that Word and renew God's covenant with them. You're not going to walk in the Word of God, which is the Covenant of God to you, until you give yourself up and over to God! You have got to want God and His will (His Covenant) more than you want food or necessaries or popularity.

The scripture in Matthew 6:33 teaches us to "seek ye first the kingdom of God and His righteousness and all these things (necessities) will be added unto you."

Separation

Separation from strangers or the world's influences in other words those influences that are not in line with the covenant of God. Separation is an outward thing but a practical side of sanctification. In verses two-three, the seed of Israel, the true heirs of God separated themselves from all strangers.

In New Testament terms we would call these individuals as those who are born again, believers or saved people. The term strangers here is indicative of worldly influence. You can't obey God and His Word and the world's wisdom at the same time, you have got to separate one from the other. The believer needs to make up his mind which position is more important, God's word or the world's wisdom. It is inferred from Israel's confession that they had been going the way of the strangers' words when they confessed their sins. They saw the way of the stranger's wisdom was wrong.

Real confession involves forsaking and coming out of the world's system and thinking and its way of doing things. Israel stood in their places as repented covenant people. They read the Book one fourth of the day and another fourth of the day they confessed and worshiped God. When you get serious with God and His word and real sanctification and separation takes place, you will get serious about Bible reading, confession and worshiping God and committed to walking in the word.

Servants

Servants who lead in walking in the Word (Covenant). In verses four and five, it gives a list of Levites who led in causing Israel to walk in the word. These Levites were examples to others that the word they had re-discovered was real and that God was real and that they would call on Him as the people looked on! They would lead as servants of the most high God. We must have men and women in our local assemblies that would show to this untoward generation, this perverse nation; with its low morals and laxed ethics and degenerate lifestyles…that there are still remnants that want to live in the Word that God has given them. Sinners, lukewarm and carnal Christians need to see that there are those of us who still respect the Word of God and have set our hearts and will to follow that word.

As we lead in the walk in the Word, it will cause conviction to take place and others will join in the walk. Everybody can't sit back and talk about how good the Word is, how it sounds good and say I believe it might work! No, no, we need those who would lead to practice the Words of the Covenant. Let's show this dying, sighing, troubled and tormented world that the Word works!

Surveying

Surveying Gods' goodness toward Israel. From verses 6-31, shows how good God had been to Israel in spite of their failures and disobedience toward Him. As the Levites were calling on the name of the Lord and blessing Him and exalting His name above any and everything else that could be praised—they begin to survey, that is to bring back to their memory/mind just how good God had been to them and acknowledge the fact that He was still good to them and was worthy of their trust now.

From verses 6-31 reading randomly, we see the Levites recalling Gods' dealings with Israel beginning with Abram (from UR and changing his name to Abraham) ending with them slaying the messengers who warned them of their sins and encouraged them to repent. The Levites recalled that God had given the land of Canaan to Abraham.

After Abrahams' death and years later, they then went to Egypt where God performed signs, wonders and miracles to deliver them out of Pharaohs' hands. God delivered them through the Red Sea. The same sea that they were delivered through; drowned their enemies.

God led them by a certain cloud in the sky by day and a pillar of fire in the sky by night to give them direction as to where to go. On Mount Sinai, He gave them His laws, His statues, His Judgements, His Sabbaths, and His commandments to follow so as to please Him. They recalled that God had given them bread for their hunger and water from a rock for their thirst and encouraged them to go in and possess the land that He had sworn to give them. Instead of Israel following the Lords' leadings, they rebelled against God and hardened their necks against Him.

Verse 17 tells us that they refused to obey and had forgotten all the miracles that God had performed before them. They were so rebellious that they appointed a captain to lead them in returning to Egypt! They had made themselves a molten calf and claimed "it" to be the god that brought them out of Egypt.

Looking back and seeing where Israel was now, the Levites acknowledged God as a God who was ready to pardon, gracious and merciful, slow to anger and of great kindness. They acknowledged that God did not turn His back on them in the wilderness nor forsake them in their rebellious state. God did not even remove the clouds by day and by night that guided them.

Verse 20 shows us that Gods' spirit continued to be among them to instruct them and did not withhold the manna (food) that He had provided for them, nor did He withhold water from them. Verse 21 shows that he kept them while they were in the wilderness for forty years. They lacked nothing, their clothes did not wear out nor did their feet swell. They had no need for another pair of shoes! After the wilderness situation, verses 22-25, He gave them kingdoms and nations subduing kings, taking their lands, capturing strong cities. The Israelites took possessions, houses and drank from wells they did not dig. The Lord multiplied their seeds as He brought them into the land of Canaan.

From verses 26-30, Israel experienced an off and on relationship with God even after He had showered them with His goodness and mercies. These verses reflected their behavior and actions forgetting what the Lord had done for them. Israel rebelled against the Lords' ways and God gave them over to those who would trouble them. Israel even killed the prophets who were sent to them to correct them. When Israel repented, He sent them deliverers. Every time they returned to God, He would bless them and then they would rebel again. This pattern of events continued. In verse 31, they recognized that God had been good to them. They admitted that for His great mercy's sake, He did not utterly consume them nor forsook them, for He is a gracious and merciful God!

The Levites surveyed God's goodness, His "track" record (if you will) to the seed of Israel. They recognized (verses 32-38) that God was just in His dealings with them. They had caused the troubles which fell upon them. In verse 36, they confessed to God that they were slaves in the land that He had given to them and their forefathers to eat of its produce. But because of their sins, the kings that the Lord had placed over them, the abundant harvest that the land produced is enjoyed by their captors. The oppressors now ruled over their bodies, their cattle and their possessions to do whatever they pleased, and now the Lords' people were under distress. The Levites expressed to God, knowing how good the

Lord had been to them, that the leaders, priests and the other Levites were going to put in writing; affixing/sealing their names to an agreement (a sure covenant) that they would follow the Lord!

The devil doesn't want the believer to walk in the Word of God. The enemy tries to tell us that God is not good and that He is not faithful! But I dare you to "check Him out", you will discover that He's all of that and more! The scripture says in psalms, "O taste and see that the Lord is good." God is good to us and as long as we walk in the Word, we will be blessed. And, yet when we miss the mark, He is still faithful with chastisement as a loving father would give to his child to get us back in line with His Word. You had better look back over your life and see how good the Lord has been to you, even when you know you didn't deserve His goodness. You-believers ought to be counted in the number and say like the Levites and the others, I will walk in the Word of God and will make a re-commitment to Him to do His bidding. In short, say," I will Refocus and Maintain my focus on the Lord."

Saints Sealed

These were the believers that signed an agreement saying they were committed to walk in the Word-the Covenant of God. At the end of the servants' discourse, after setting themselves apart, cleansing themselves and acknowledging Gods' goodness, they recommitted themselves to the Word of God that was already given to them through Moses. They said we will make a "sure" covenant -what I believe to mean is; we will follow the Word with our actions and not just with our mouths.

This is a good thing for us to remember as New Testament believers, that we should commit ourselves to obeying the already written and known Word of God. We should return to the old landmarks of the Bible. We don't need to add or take away anything in the Word of God. The Apostle Paul has instructed us in the book of Timothy 2:15 to rightly divide the Word of God. We should not allow any obstacle to get in the way of truth. If we follow Pauls' instruction, we will limit ourselves with the errors that are so frequently found in the body of Christ.

These that I call sealed saints would affix their names to the Covenant that they agreed to walk in. In the New Testament oftentimes believers are called saints. The term carries the dual connotation of being set apart to God and partaking of His holiness. Those thus called saints are not automatically holy in character, but they are urged to live according to their holy position.

From Nehemiah chapter 10:1-29, it tells us who signed the covenant with their names and said that they would walk in it. Have fun trying to pronounce the entire list of names! Like these believers who went "public" with God, it's time for the saints under the New Testament Covenant to come out of the "closet" and come clean with God. We should write our names down as a representative of the covenant, saying we will follow and live out the Word of God. We ought not be ashamed of the Gospel of Jesus Christ. In the Gospel you can be saved, spared, sealed, strengthened, sanctified and separated! We ought to let others know you stand for the Covenant-The Word of God and that you are sealed with the precious blood of Jesus Christ! As a born-again believer, you are already sealed with the precious Holy Spirit of Promise, now you must seal yourself to keep the book that's already written for saved-sealed saints.

Stipulations of the Covenant

Verse 29 shows the earnestness, the realness and when they gave to support the house of God. Further stipulations are seen in verse 34, which included bringing wood to the house of authenticity in entering into this covenant with each other and with God. They bound themselves to a curse and unto an oath to walk in God's Law and to do what He had commanded. The sealed saints agreed to walk in "ALL" the commandments. They were not going to pick and choose some of the commandments to obey and omit others. This is done too often in todays' church. We obey some of the "milk" of the word which does not cost us very much to obey but when it comes to obeying the "meat" of the word, we choose not to obey because it causes us to make sacrifices.

In the Covenant, verse 30, the people stipulated that they would not give their daughters and sons in marriage to the heathens. In our todays' vernacular the heathens would be the unsaved person. That is to someone who did not believe in God and had not received Jesus as their savior, then this couple would be unequally yoked. They also stipulated in verse 31, that they would keep the Sabbath-the Lords' appointed rest day holy. And they would abide by its ordinances of not buying or selling anything on the Sabbath day. They would forgo the seventh year and cancel all debts if they were owed money by anyone among themselves.

In verse 32, Israel committed to giving a portion of their increase to take care of the expenses of the house of God. In that season of history, verse 33 lists the things that the people would be helping with God so that it would be burned on the altar of the Lord. From verses 35-37, the people pledged to put God first in their giving. They would give of all their substances which included first fruits, the dedication of their first born and giving and bringing of their tithes to the Levites as the priests looked on, verse 38. All their giving expressed in verse 39, was done so that the house of the Lord would not be neglected or forsaken in any way.

As a pastor/leader of a local assembly, it's my desire that every New Testament believer take hold of these commitments/stipulations as well. All New Testament believers should be walking in covenant with God, not necessarily like those in our text, but nevertheless in covenant with God. A covenant is an agreement between two persons. Both parties have responsibility. If one does his part, then the other party has the responsibility to do his part. In the book of Hebrews chapter eight, God has given us (New Testament believers) a "new covenant" with better promises than those in the Old Testament covenant.

Some of their covenant stipulations we are admonished to follow as well. Things like putting people in place to carry out the work of God, families coming together and living holy, setting aside a sabbath of sorts to worship, taking care of the house of God and putting God first in our giving. These things that Nehemias' Israel followed, would do those of us in the body of Christ well if we performed them.

In the work of the ministry and of the house of God, the support and resources to take care of the house of God should not be left to a few believers. If you are a part of a local assembly, you should take on the responsibility to share in the care and expenses of the house of God and the work of God. We must remember as New Testament believers; we can't do the work of God the way we want to but rather how God has ordered us to do so.

We must function according to the written stipulations of the Word of God. We need not add or take away from the Bible. If we stay with the Bible, we will be alright. Why don't you make the commitment that you are going to walk in the Word, the covenant that God has given to us? Let us refocus on the Word of God and maintain that focus by walking and being committed to that written word.

Selected Saints

From chapter 11, we will see a number of individuals that were selected to live in the city of Jerusalem. The walls had been rebuilt and the gates had been repaired. Various leading individuals had built their homes in Jerusalem and lived there while others built their homes outside of the city on lands of their inheritance. It appears that more inhabitants were needed to occupy/dwell in the capital city. Their private houses were spatially separated from one another. More inhabitants were needed in Jerusalem for protection and for the work that would take place concerning the house of God.

To further populate Jerusalem with more inhabitants, verse 1-2, a lot was casted as a means to select who would be the other occupants in the city. From each tribe only one out of ten would be selected to live in the city of Jerusalem. Those who were willing and selected to live in Jerusalem received the blessings of the people.

Casting a "lot" was a practice that was allowed by God especially in the Old Testament and a few times in the New Testament before the death of Jesus brought about a new covenant. The casting of lots helped in the decision-making process and to determine duties. The casting of "lots" is most often compared to our modern-day version of flipping a coin or drawing names out of a hat. As New Testament Christians we are not instructed to cast lots as a way to know God's will. New Testament believers have the Holy Spirit living in them and we have the Word of God to guide us and to understand the will of God for our lives. However, "casting lots" was the case in the text setting under consideration.

From the text of this chapter including verses 3-36, it gives the various names and the numbers of those who lived in Jerusalem as well as the additional ones selected to live in the city. The dwellers in Jerusalem included priests, Levites, Solomon's servants, workers in and on the house of God and certain singers who were commanded by the king to be singers.

Sacred Saints

Chapter twelve of Nehemiah beginning with verse 1 and going to verse 26, gives the names of the priests and the Levites who had come to Jerusalem earlier under the leadership of Zerubbabel, Jeshua, Seraiah, Jeremiah and Ezra. These men are who I called, Sacred Saints because they do the work of God in and around the house of God.

The priest would represent their people before God in things pertaining to God. They would offer both gifts and sacrifices for sins. They would also teach the Laws of God to the people. They would often determine whether a person was sick or healthy. The Levites are the tribe whose men serve as priests, to a large degree the terms of priests and Levites are interchangeable. They are organized into units in order to carry out the various holy duties assigned to them. The Levites performed work related to the tent of meetings and its utensils. Additional duties of the Levites included breaking down and setting up of the camps as they moved to various places in their journey, kindling fires, washing linens, butchering animals and processing grains. In general, their work was to assist all of Israel in serving God and doing His will. The work of the priest and the Levites was their permanent career.

As we look back over the outline, let us implement these S's in our lives. We should sanctify ourselves to God wholly and holy and submit to Him forever. We are to be separated from any influences that would hinder our walk with God. We must realize as blood-bought sons and daughters that we are servants of the most high God. As servants, we must continually survey (look back over our lives) to see where God has brought us from.

As Christians we should be committed to walking out the word of God in our lives. The word of God stipulated how we are to live our lives as pleasing unto God. Remember every New Testament believer has been chosen as (selected and sacred) workers in holiness and in the fear of God. Our work and service for the Lord should be considered as sacred and should be our permanent careers like those of old as well, regardless of what our positions are in the body of Christ.

Chapter 11

Nehemiah 12:27-31
THANKING AND PRAISING GOD FOR WHAT HE HAS DONE

In our study of this powerful book of Nehemiah, allow me to go back for a bit of refreshment so we can flow with the content in a continuous manner as we embark upon this latter part of chapter twelve. Nehemiah was concerned about the state of affairs in Jerusalem. God used him to go to Jerusalem (while in captivity under the Babylonian rule) with the king's permission and resources to rebuild walls that had been destroyed during the Babylonian defeat of Israel almost seventy years earlier. With a God focus for Israel and with singleness of heart, he moved forward in restoring the walls and gates of Jerusalem.

Nehemiah immediately met opposition while seeking to obey God in rebuilding the walls and gates. He had opposition from without and he had opposition from within. In every trial and test, God allowed him to prevail as he prayed and got wisdom from God on how to handle the opposition. In record time, fifty-two days, the walls were rebuilt. The opposition recognized that the work was wrought by the hands of God.

Nehemiah began to re-organize Jerusalem because the people were out of order. The people that were not true Israelites and their names could not be found in the register were not allowed to serve. The word of God was rediscovered as it had been neglected. The people did what they thought was right in their own eyes. Nehemiah knew that if there would be consistent purity and order, it must be done based on the word of God.

The people respected the word of God as they stood up when it was read. They found out some things that they should be doing, and they started practicing these things. Because of their willingness to obey the word of the Lord, there was great joy and gladness among themselves. When the word was rediscovered, there were those who was so excited, so committed to following the word of the Lord and renewing their covenant with God, they signed their names in a binding oath that they would walk in the word of God and that they would be committed to walk in the covenant.

You recall that in chapter eleven, Nehemiah recognizes that all of Israel would not be able to live in Jerusalem. Jerusalem was the chief city of Israel where the walls and gates had been recently repaired. Even though all had worked on the rebuilt walls and gates in Jerusalem, everyone would not be able to live in the chief city. There would be those who lived in Jerusalem and there would be those who lived in the cities of their inheritances. One tenth of Israel was required to live in Jerusalem and the rest of the people resided in the land around Jerusalem which was resettled by the people and some of the priests. The names of the authentic priests and some Levites were listed with their rights, responsibilities and the respect that was to be given to them.

Focus had brought Israel to some finished goals. Focus had caused them to be faithful. Refocusing had caused them to renew their covenant with God. Maintaining focus had caused them to stay motivated and keep that momentum to complete the monumental task of rebuilding the walls and gates of Jerusalem and setting the house of Israel and the house of God in order. The culmination of the work was to be celebrated in dedicating the walls and gates to the glory of God.

To God be the glory for the great things He has done! Israel would be giving God thanks and praise for what he has done. Every time you Think, you ought to Thank! They recognized that it was God who brought about the victory. It was incumbent and necessary upon Israel to give God the glory, honor and praise due to Him for what He had done. They realized that they could not have completed God's work without the help of the Lord. God will help those of us who He had commissioned to work for Him, He will not leave us alone to complete the assignments He has for our lives. Our responsibility is to be willing and obedient to follow His every instruction.

As we began to look at chapter twelve, verse twenty-seven, Israel was to keep the dedication of the walls with gladness both with thanksgiving and with singing. God wanted both the thanksgiving and the singing. They were to use musical instruments in thanking and praising God. So much for the saying, "you don't use musical instruments in worshiping and praising God!"

When God blesses you, causes you to triumph, causes you to gain, to prosper you, gives you victory, takes care of you and provides for you, etc., you ought to stop and give Him thanks and praise for the wonderful things He has done for you. It's not that I must thank and praise Him, but rather you should show Him how grateful you are for the marvelous and wonderful things He has done for you. You show that by giving Him thanksgiving and praise. I don't believe we are radical enough with our thanksgiving and praise toward God.

I believe we should be leaping, shouting, clapping, dancing and giving God thanks and praise publicly. If God was not ashamed to bless us, we ought not be ashamed to bless Him publicly for the good things He has done and His faithfulness toward us despite who may be looking at us and criticizing our praise. It's time to go public with Jesus! A lot of individuals have come out of the "closet". It's time for the Christian to come out of the closet with your praise for the Lord if you haven't done so already!

Saints we need to thank God and praise Him for He is worthy of all our praises from the rising of the sun to the going down of the same, His name is to be praised in all generations. There is a saying that some of us have heard, "when the praises go up, the blessing comes down." I believe this to be a true saying, so Hallelujah, praise God!

Let me remind us, before you think all there is to giving God thanksgiving and praise with singing, just using our physical bodies to do so is not all there is to thanking and praising God. The scriptures remind us that true thanksgiving, praise and worship comes out of a sanctified heart/life.

I believe in the remainder of this text, I see and want to point out three things that alert us in knowing what God wants out of us as it relates to true thanksgiving, praise and worship being given up to Him and that which He receives. We do want Him to receive our thanksgiving and praise, don't we? These three points begin with the letter "S" again perhaps for easy remembrance.

God Wants Sanctified Lives from Us

We saw in the last presentation that before Israel renewed the covenant with God, they sanctified themselves with fasting and confessions of sin and forsaking those confessed sins. Here in the text, when Israel was getting ready to dedicate the rebuilt walls with gladness and with thanksgiving and singing, verse 30 tells us the people sanctified/purified themselves. From the priests, the Levites and the people, they purified themselves and they even purified the walls and the gates. They sanctified themselves, they emptied themselves of impurities they had in their lives. Anything contaminated must go. They would purify themselves; they would place their filthy garments on the altar of God and allow God to replace their filthy garments with the garments of praise. They gave themselves totally to God. They realized that there would not be true thanksgiving and singing if they did not give themselves first to God. Ecclesiastes 9:8 says, "Let thy garments be always white; and let thy head lack no ointment."

We are to live a clean sanctified life, symbolized by wearing white garments. Ointment on our heads symbolizes an anointed life full of the spirit of God. We are deceived to think God is receiving our worship and praise from us when we are living unholy lifestyles, when our garments are dirty and no anointing in our lives. The elements of wearing a white garment and having ointment on our heads shows our intimate connection and fellowship with God. We all must be about this sanctified process of becoming more and more like the Lord.

In the sanctified process under discussion, Nehemiah, in verse 31-42, appointed two large companies of men who would give thanks to God as noted in verse 40 and the location on the wall of each appointed group. One company of praisers was gathered with Nehemiah on parts of the finished wall and the other company on the other side of the finished wall. The priests used the instruments of David and the trumpets to praise God, verse 41.

These sanctified singers, verse 42, sang loud and offered their praise, thanksgiving and worship up to God. True thanksgiving always involves giving yourself first to God. According to Romans 12:1, the writer tells us to" present ourselves, bodies, to God as a living sacrifice, holy and acceptable unto God which is our reasonable service." God wants all our faculties committed to Him while we give thanksgiving and praise to Him. If He is going to receive our thanksgiving and praise from us, we must meet His requirements.

God Wants Sacrificial Giving Offerings from Us

Not only do we give ourselves to God, which is first and foremost, but we give of our substances as well when we are thankful. In true Thanksgiving, you give. At this dedication, the people gave sacrificially; the scripture says they offered "great sacrifices." No doubt their sacrificial offerings included their best animals, their best food from their crops, they gave their silver and gold. They gave what was precious and meaningful to them. They gave back to God to show Him their thanksgiving for what He had done for them. The question that is asked of us is, what do we give? A second question for you to consider is this, can you be thankful to God and rob Him of our substances?

We give our treasures, our time and talents to Him. Our treasures include our monies, our tithes and offerings. We should give God our time. We must set aside time to be alone with Him in reading the word, in prayer and in meditation. We must acknowledge Him in everything that we do. We give back to God any talents He has bestowed upon us to use for His glory and honor. Our gifts and talents are given to us by God, and He will anoint them for His glory. He puts Himself on that talent/gift to do what we couldn't do without Him! That's why we should give out talents back to God for His use.

When Israel showed their thanksgiving with their "great sacrifices", they did it from a cheerful heart and they gave liberally. They did not feel the compulsion to give but gave willingly and cheerfully. The scripture says in verse 43b, c, they rejoiced for God had made them rejoice with great joy.

God will bless us when we delight ourselves in Him and obey Him. He will cause rejoicing in us! Could your lack of rejoicing be due to the fact that you are not giving sacrificially, obeying Him and delighting yourself in Him?

The spirit of joy was so contagious that not only did the men rejoice, but the whole household got in on the rejoicing! The wives and the children rejoiced so much so that the joy of Jerusalem was heard even afar off! This was an awesome time of thanksgiving, worship and praise. When you are truly thankful, it will show up in your sacrificial giving and then you won't have to manufacture a pseudo joy—God will give you JOY!

God Wants Service from the Saints

According to verse 44, when there is true gladness and thanksgiving, there will be sanctification, sacrificial giving and service from the saints. There were appointments made to perform different services. There were those appointed over the chambers for the various offerings including first fruits and tithes that were to come in. Certain portions were gathered from the fields for the priest and the Levites.

When Judah (the tribe whose name means praise) recognized that order was taking place as the priests were getting in the correct position, they rejoiced. In other words, they did what they were known for—that is to praise God! There is not an exhaustive list of servants presented here in the text, but other individuals like the singers and porters, kept the word of their God and words of the purification according to the commandment of David and Solomon, his son. The singers lead in songs of praise and thanksgiving unto God. Daily portions for livelihood were given out to those singers, priests and Levites who served in their capacity. I would suppose this act of supplying for the needs of these certain servants in

Israel, would be equivalent to our full-time paid staff members in our local assemblies.

God wants us to praise Him, thank Him and worship Him. He inhabits the praises of His people. To know God in a personal way is to worship Him and to praise Him. When He appeared to Bible saints, they usually fell at His feet in adoration, reverence and worship. The Apostle John in the book of Revelation is a good example of when a person meets the risen Lord, one will fall at His feet to worship Him. We ought to be thankful for all that God has done for us as well as what He will be doing for us in our future.

One of the last day sins in perilous time according to the book of Timothy will be the sin of un-thankfulness! We should praise, honor and worship God for all that He has done. I assure you; you won't be able to remember and know all that He has done for you! So, praise Him for what you do know and remember. No one should make you, beg or embarrass you into praising and giving Him thanks. He deserves our praise whether you want to give it to Him or not. It is a commandment that we should give Him thanks. Remember in your thanksgiving and praising God, don't forget He wants us to live clean sanctified lives, to give sacrificially and to serve fervently.

Chapter 12

Nehemiah 13:1-9
MAINTAINING PURITY

In the text you will learn that Nehemiah had left Jerusalem after having been there for twelve years carrying out Gods' assignment for his life. Chapter 1:1 and chapter 2:1 shows us that he left Persia the 20th year and left Jerusalem in the 32nd year. This duration gives us the time he spent in Jerusalem. After returning to Persia, he only stayed there for a while before getting permission once again from the king to return to Jerusalem.

For twelve years as a leader and governor, he led Israel in the rebuilding of the walls and gates of the city. He helped to set in order the nation and its' pure walk before the God of Israel. He encouraged and emphasized the need of returning to the word of God (the covenant) of which Israel did. Various individuals were put in authentic strategic positions to carry out tasks needed to restore the nation's order. In reviewing Israel's' situation up to the time of this text, I contend at least in theory; the context forthcoming really should not have happened. Why? Because Nehemiah had left the nation of Israel in purity based on the word of God. They should have maintained the holy places that they had advanced to. Nehemiah left Jerusalem going back to Babylon focused and had maintained his singleness toward God and the work discharged to him by God. As stated, he had left Israel in purity, they were functioning in the word of God under proper authority. Undoubtedly, Nehemiah thought Israel was focused just as he was and that they were maintaining a consistent walk before God when he left Jerusalem. His desire for Israel's walk, and purity for the Lord was short lived.

No pastor or leader wants to leave the fellowship for any amount of time when there is little or no purity in the camp. This leader realizes that when he/she returns to the assembly, there will probably be more chaos and confusion that will have to be dealt with. You must know that just because you teach or preach something once or because you have exposed the people to a teaching, it doesn't mean that you won't have to go back and reteach it again. Repetition is one way a teaching is reinforced for maximum benefits. This scenario happened to Nehemiah, and it caused him to revisit what he had taught among the people. He had left Jerusalem focused and maintaining his focus before Israel had gotten out of focus, out of purity in the short period of time since his departure.

On Nehemiah's return to Jerusalem, he found out some things regarding the condition of Israel. In chapter 13:1, Nehemiah read to the audience the words from the book of Moses, and they found out that it was written that the Moabites and the Ammonites should not come into the congregation of God forever.

Verse two gives the reason that the Moabites and the Ammonites were not to have a part in Israel. When Israel had left Egypt going to the promised land and Israel needed food and water, these two groups of people would not provide these necessities to them. Instead, these two foreign nations hired one of Israel's prophets to curse Israel. The Moabites nor the Ammonites got what they wanted concerning Israel. Israel was not cursed, but rather they were blessed as God turned that potential curse into a blessing!

How many of you can testify that what the enemy meant for your harm, God turned it around for your good? Why? Because He is the God of the "turn around." He will turn your situation around, your circumstances, your dilemmas and your destruction into a blessing. Joseph learned what the devil meant for harm/evil to him as the devil used his brothers against him, God turned his situation around and caused Joseph to occupy the second highest position in the land of Egypt.

When the law against the Moabites and the Ammonites was read, verse three, the people once again under the leadership of Nehemiah began to separate themselves from the mixed multitude. The mixed multitude were those who had no part of the covenant of Israel nor any inheritance among them.

If you recall, just a little time ago the word of God was read to Israel in a marathon manner by Ezra. The details in the word were consistent with what they were doing now by separating themselves from these two groups of people. At the time of Ezra's reading, those excited hearers made an oath in Chapter 10:29 and put themselves under a curse that they would walk in the word of God. These hearers signed their names to keep the covenant. The oath stated that they would not give their sons and daughters to be married to foreigners. Also, that they would keep the Sabbath, take care of the house of God, that they would bring and give the tithes and offerings and do everything else the law commanded.

Israel had broken their oath with God and had allowed themselves to fall back into a place where they had once been before Nehemiah's first visit. Did Israel really think they were walking in purity by practicing things against the covenant of God? Maybe Israel thought they were, but the careful reader of the text knows that they weren't keeping the covenant. They had broken all the tenets of their oaths to follow the Lord. Nehemiah had left Jerusalem to return to Persia as he had promised the king. So, when Nehemiah left, Israel laxed back into impurity and out of covenant order. They now needed to be separated from that mixed multitude and get back to spiritual purity.

Believers don't fool yourselves; the mixed multitude will cause trouble. Those who don't have the mind of Christ and carry a different message and a way of living can and most assuredly turn you from God's way of doing things. One can see this kind of departure from God clearly with King Solomon. Solomon was one of the greatest kings of Israel but allowed himself to be tempted and lured into marriages and unions with a mixed multitude of women. The entrapment of these women caused his heart to turn away from God. Israel now had to be purified once again because of their compromise with the mixed multitude.

In verse four, we are reintroduced to the high priest, Eliashib. He was introduced to us in chapter 3:1 where he and his priestly brethren were busy in building the sheepgate and sanctifying it. Eliashib had the oversight (the care, the responsibility) of the chamber of the house of God. The priest, Eliashib, had a situation however! He was allied to Tobiah. Remember him? Tobiah had given Nehemiah much trouble.

Tobiah is mentioned with others who in chapter 2:19, laughed and scorned and despised Nehemiah's efforts to rebuild the walls of Jerusalem and he also accused him of rebelling against the king. In chapter 4:3,7, he criticized the strength of the walls that were being built and stated that if a fox went up on the wall it would collapse. In verse seven, he was angry that Nehemiah was bridging gaps in the walls and that Nehemiah did not stop building because of the ridicule herald at him by Tobiah and his partners. In chapter 6:5,17, Tobiah was a part of the open letter writing campaign to stop Nehemiah's progress. And, in verse 17, Tobiah was corresponding in letters with nobles in Jerusalem and they did in turn communicate with him in letters. Letters were written to Nehemiah telling him of the good deeds Tobiah had done for

Judah. Tobiah sent letters to Nehemiah to put fear in him. In all these references, Tobiah was causing Nehemiah and Israel some kinds of trouble even though some of the people were deceived by his character and they dismissed what the word had said about Tobiah and his ancestry.

Nehemiah had properly discerned Tobiah and his worth to Israel. Nehemiah knew Tobiah's ancestry; that he was an Ammonite. Because he was an Ammonite, he was not to have any inheritance in Israel at all! The focused leader already knew what the word had said on the subject concerning Tobiah and his ancestry based on Deuteronomy 23:3-4, it says, "an Ammonite or Moabite shall not enter into the congregation of the Lord; even to their tenth generation shall they not enter into the congregation of the Lord forever: because they met you not with bread and with water in the way, when ye came forth out of Egypt; and because they hired against thee Balaam the son of Beor of Pethor of Mesopotamia to curse thee."

Nehemiah knew God's decision to exclude the Ammonites and the Moabites among Israel and Judah knew it as well. The law had been read and explained to them prior to Nehemiah's initial visit to Jerusalem and read to them while he was there in Jerusalem for those twelve years. Nehemiah would not compromise the word and had spoken out against Tobiah telling him in chapter 2:20c, that he had no portion, nor rights nor memorial in Jerusalem as he rebuked Tobiah.

But now, the high priest had made an alliance with Tobiah. The priest had compromised the word. The word was ignored regarding the Amorites and the Moabites being a part of Israel's worship and their covenant relationship with God. The congregation compromised as well as they should not have allowed Eliashib to do what he had done for Tobiah. The congregation of Israel knew why God had forbidden the

Ammonites and the Moabites from being connected to them, but they refused to comply with God's commandment.

What did Eliashib, the high priest, do for Tobiah? Verse 7, indicates to us that the priest had made Tobiah a "great chamber." The place where the chamber was built was to be used for the frankincense, the vessels of God, the meat offerings, the place where the tithe of the corn was to be stored and where oil and wine was kept. Eliashib had defiled the chamber in the house of God by building a place of residency for Tobiah in that sacred place.

Nehemiah, verse six, informed the reader that he was not in Jerusalem when the high priest consented to this ungodly action. Nehemiah had returned to Babylon and shortly after he obtained permission to return to Jerusalem. What things the people will do when the leader is present let alone when he/she is not present!

Compromise had brought impurity into the house of God. The compromise was evil, and it was not in right standing with the word of God. Nehemiah knew if there was no purity, there would be no power. If there was no holiness, there would be no hollowness and the people would end up back in the shape that he found them in years earlier.

Many of us know better than to compromise, we know what the word says about sanctification and holiness and go right on and compromise. When we compromise, we lose our purity and holiness and dare anyone to say anything about our condition. Often the person goes on in their perspective position among the pews without repenting, lessening the power of God in that assembly. We must know that our behavior does affect others around us.

If the church would be a powerful tool/vessel in the hands of God, we must keep purity in the place, holiness in the house, sanctification in the sanctuary, temperance in the temple, power in the pew and Christ in the church. Purity and power go together and is the mark of distinction for the believer. When we lose our purity, the glory will depart. The word "cabod" means glory and "ichabod" means the glory has departed. When the "I" gets in front of the cabod, you will have Ichabod. For whatever reason, when the "I" gets its way in the front of God's glory, the glory of God will leave.

It is not known for sure, but there is a hint in chapter 6:18-19 that maybe the reason why Eliashib did this terrible thing of building a dwelling place for Tobiah in the house of God was because Tobiah was in the priests' family through marriage or because he had done a great deed for the priest. Nevertheless, Eliashib had allowed impurity to come into Israel and Israel broke their covenant of being pure before God.

Verse seven tells us that focused Nehemiah heard what Eliashib had done in preparing a dwelling place in the chamber courts of the house of God for Tobiah. He understood what Eliashib had done was evil based on the word of God. Someone may have said to Nehemiah, "all you are doing is nitpicking, you are just trying to find something to stir up trouble over." Another one could have said, "leave Tobiah alone, he's a good man and has done a lot of good deeds for Israel", yet another one may have said, "he is one of us, he has relatives among us by marriage." I can still hear in my mind someone else saying, "Nehemiah, all you are interested in is focus, refocusing and maintaining focus, purity, order, commitment and continuous righteousness." I like to think that Nehemiah answered back and said, "you are so right, I am interested in all the things you have said!"

Nehemiah knew what the word of God had said on the subject, and he was not about to compromise that word. He further realized that Israel had come from rubbish, ruin and rottenness to being a blessed bunch! Their blessings were because of obeying the words of the Lord and not compromising them. Nehemiah was determined that he would not go in the path of his fellow kinsmens through compromise. The focused leader knew if Israel would not obey the word of God, it would not be long before they were back in ruins and once more become a reproach unto God. Nehemiah wanted to restore purity, peace and power back in the place.

Nehemiah expressed godly anger and grief over what Eliashib, and Israel had done since he had left Jerusalem and now returned. Verse eight states that the actions especially of Eliashib in building Tobiah a dwelling place in God's house caused Nehemiah to sorely grieve. Nehemiah had a righteous attitude over the sins that were being committed against God, sins that were to the hurt of Israel. What is alarming was the fact that others saw and knew what was happening; the sins being committed but no one did anything about it.

Like Jesus who expressed righteous indignation when the people were selling and trading things in the house of God, He cast out and overturned the tables of the money changers in the temple. And so, Nehemiah's righteous indignation caused him to cast out all of Tobiah's belongings out of the chamber! Nehemiah broke up Tobiah's "playhouse" as Tobiah had no place or portion nor inheritance or memorial in Jerusalem.

With strong authority, Nehemiah commanded that the place where Tobiah had dwelled be cleansed. Notice he did not suggest it be cleansed but rather commanded it to be cleansed. Sometimes the leader must use his strong authority invested in him by God to get the Lord's house back in order and in purity, especially when sin goes unchecked and not dealt with. The chamber was to be restored back to its proper purpose and place. The vessels of God were returned to their rightful place along with the meat offerings and the frankincense. There will be purity in the house when the word of God is obeyed.

We must maintain purity in the house of God-our churches. Purity is not only to be experienced when we come to church, but it must affect every area of our lives every day! God knows when our purity is real. He knows the fake, the sham and every plaything we call holiness. We can grin, cry, shout, holler and run around the sanctuary to fool others regarding our lack of purity and holiness but you can't fool God at any time or with anything. Our mandate is clear and concise, we have got to be clean before the living Christ. If we are out of focus, we must refocus and then maintain that focus of purity and order. We must come out of our dungeons of darkness, our bowels of bondages and our personal prisons. We must not allow our flesh to do what it thinks is right in its eyes. Know that when there is no order or purity God wants to restore His people who are called by His name. He has a purpose that He has called each one of us to. We must constantly remind ourselves that we are a holy people, a peculiar people, a royal priesthood that should show forth His praises. We are sanctified vessels full of "sacrificial stuff and a good smelling order!"

We can't allow that which God rejects to take up residence in our temples-that is our bodies. The Tobiah's we compromise with in this world is not worth us/you losing our/your anointing over. The scripture teaches us in a powerful way that those who know God, depart from sin and be pure, be holy and be clean. The scriptures further teach us that those who bear the ark of the Lord, must have clean hands and a clean heart. Anything that is opposed to the will of God for your life, must be laid daily at the feet of Jesus where we die daily. We should have a funeral with our sin(s) each day that they occur. We are bond slaves to Jesus Christ, and we must move at His commands.

If you are a part of the body of Christ, but you are stinking up the world with your sins, we must quickly run to God's altar where we are altered. Allow the Holy Spirit to pour out on you a fresh anointing as the heat is turned up on that altar where your flesh begins to die. The only problem with a living sacrifice (Romans 12) is the sacrifices keep climbing off or jumping down from the altar. As the heat is turned up to burn up the junk in their lives and they begin to stink in the dying process, many living sacrifices can't stand the heat of the call and they "flesh out." Our flesh will fight against order and purity. The flesh doesn't want perimeters, pens nor boundaries. The flesh wants to do its own thing and not from the Holy Ghost. When this occurs, there will be chaos and confusion. Be it known that God is not the author of confusion. So, let us as God's people maintain purity so that God would be honored, and we would be blessed.

Chapter 13

Nehemiah 13:10-31

MAINTAINING ORDER IN THE HOUSE

As you recall in the last chapter, Nehemiah had previously gone back to Babylon for a short period of time as he had promised the king of Persia he would return sometime later. Nehemiah had been in Jerusalem for twelve years before returning to the Shushan palace. He had left Persia in the 20th year and returned there in the 32nd year. He had previously served in Persia as a cupbearer to the king. While in Jerusalem, over the twelve years he stayed there, he had the major task of rebuilding the torn/burned walls and gates of Jerusalem. It took only 52 days to complete the work despite the opposition he faced on a daily basis. The walls and the gates were built in fifty-two days, but it took the entire twelve years he was there in Jerusalem to build the people! Lessons that Nehemiah taught Israel often had to be repeated as they would neglect or blatantly disobey the teachings and return to a selfish lifestyle.

You can build a house in perhaps a few months or even a year, but it takes a lifetime building a home. Yes, you can build a physical structure called a church in a manner of months or years, but it takes longer than that to get the churches of the Lord Jesus Christ to get in purity and order. It only takes a few minutes at a church altar or before a Justice of Peace to say, "I do", but it takes a lifetime in building that marriage.

In review, when Nehemiah left Jerusalem after being there twelve years, he had appointed and placed people in strategic positions to carry out various tasks. The word of God was rediscovered, and it was to be their final authority in practice and behavior. The walls and gates were dedicated to God's glory. Israel's covenant with God had been renewed and the people were thankful for what God had done for them and through them.

When Nehemiah returned to Jerusalem, he found out that the people had been drifting away from God and became laxed in their obedience to the word of God and now they were slipping back into bondage whether they knew it or not. The people and priests were ignoring the word of God and refusing to submit to it. As a result, they had gotten out of order. Nehemiah knew that order must be maintained. When you don't follow the "book" (the Bible) you will get out of order. When there is no order there will be no purity. If you recall in chapter eight, the chapter talked about order. Lessons taught, oftentimes, must be re-taught as we will see going forward.

You must know that when you and I don't follow the word of God; refusing to obey the word which will help us to stay clean and pure, you will find yourself back in bondages. The bondage will happen again even after you have been delivered from the very thing that is now threatening to put you back in that bondage!

Any time you get delivered from something/anything, the devil seeks to entrap, entice, tempt, tantalize and lure and lead you back into bondage again with the very thing(s) that had been destroying your life earlier.

Because the devil has been eyeing and trying to sift you like he did with Peter, he knows your weaknesses, your areas of conflict and what you wrestle and struggle with daily. Even after you have prayed, confessed your sins and even been delivered from the clutches of Satan, this devil that we face still seeks to pull you back into that thing(s) the flesh wanted and craved and lure you back into the desires/cares of the world. The flesh and the world are his territories, and he thinks he can handle you while you are there on his turf.

When Nehemiah returned to Jerusalem, he saw that Israel had refused to obey God regarding what God had said in His word dealing with the Amorites and the Moabites. These two nations of people were not to come into the congregation of God, forever. Israel had allowed the Amorites and the Moabites to intermingle with them and many of the Israelites had married some of these foreigners. Israel's purity had been threatened as purity is the mark and distinction of God's people. Without purity and holiness, God's people are no different in actions from the sinners and heathens who don't know God!

We can know the words of the scriptures, we can know the language of the church, we can know the songs of praises of the body of Christ, and we can know the structure of the church; yet have no real connection with the Lord. Things like giving, living holy, praying without ceasing and even the ministry of deliverance are often neglected and omitted among many who say they are a part of the Jesus' Church which He established. This description will be present when there is no purity and holiness in our lives. The rediscovered Word of God through Moses brought conviction upon the Israelites, and they separated themselves from all the mixed multitude. When there is no mind of Christ, the mixed multitude will offer us so many more kinds of mindsets that will get us in error from what God desires for us. Notice, some people confuse conviction with condemnation. If you are wrong in an area of your life based on what the scriptures say about that "wrongness", don't get mad or argue over the scriptures and rationalize your behavior, just repent and be changed in that area of your life.

Not only were they ignoring the word regarding the Ammonites and the Moabites, but the ignorance/neglect was expressed in a blatant way. The High Priest allied himself with Tobiah, an Ammonite, who was a known enemy (Chapter 6:16) to Nehemiah and Israel. The High Priest had built a plush/great chamber in the house of God for this man. Tobiah was given a place/position of authority that did not belong to him. God never intended for Tobiah or any other Ammonite or Moabite to have such a place in the house of God no matter what good deeds they may have done for many in Israel. The High Priest had exchanged the use of the chamber from its original function; where the meat offering, frankincense, the vessels of God, the new wine and the tithe of corn was kept and now he made Tobiah a great chamber in that holy place!

Nehemiah reminds us that he was not in Jerusalem when the High Priest built the chamber and the other going on was happening. He had returned to Babylon as he had promised the king of Persia that he would. Nehemiah left Jerusalem believing that Israel would maintain their focus order and purity, but they didn't. The old saying may prove to be true still, "while the cat (Nehemiah) is away, the mice (Israel) will play." Nehemiah came to Jerusalem, and he understood the "evil" that the High Priest had committed. It seems that sometimes "evil" is going on but not understood by the people that it is "evil", or it appears that the participants don't care that their actions are violating the word of God. The leader had to point out to these indifferent and insensitive people that evil was among them even when they did not recognize or discern it as such.

The "evil" that Nehemiah witnessed grieved him. It grieved him so much, that he did something about it! He took the initiative, the oversight and the authority like the leader should do and he cast forth all the household stuff of Tobiah

out of the house of God. Verse nine says, "then I commanded (not suggested) that the chamber be cleansed." The
chamber was restored to its proper function by the actions of
Nehemiah. He brought order back to the people of God and
to the house of God.

In verse 10, Nehemiah also perceives, (he saw, he found
out, God showed him) that portions which were supposed to
be given to the Levites and to the singers had not been given
to them. Because the Levites and the singers were not receiving their portions, it forced them to go back out to the
workplace to make money. The money gained by them
would be used to take care of themselves. God did not intend
for it to be this way concerning their welfare. God wanted
those who did the work of the Lord to be taken care of by
those whom they served. This principle is also found in the
New Testament.

In the book of First Corinthians 9:1-14, this principle is
taught but particularly verse nine, verse 13 and verse 14.
Verse nine says, "For it is written in the law of Moses, thou
shalt not muzzle the mouth of the ox that treadeth out the
corn. Doth God take care for oxen?" Verse 13 says, "Do ye
not know that they which minister about holy things live of the
things of the temple? and they which wait at the altar are par-
takers with the altar?" Verse 14 says, "Even so hath the Lord
ordained that they which preach the gospel should live of the
gospel." Those who are in ministry positions doing work for
the Lord, they should be taken care of by those whom they
serve.

Verse 11 shows us that Nehemiah confronted/contended
with the rulers asking them why they were neglecting the
house of God by their actions? Nehemiah gathered the rulers
together and put them in their places! Verse 12 seems to indicate to us that after Nehemiah confronted the people, their
actions were seen as they returned what belonged to God's

house back to the house of God. The people were withholding the tithes of corn and new wine for themselves, and they returned the tithes back to Gods' established treasuries. In this Nehemiah setting, to rob God of the tithe would bring on a curse. The God robbers would be cursed with a curse. Their robbery was just another indication that the people had gotten out of the order of God.

Verse 13 is interesting to note as you compare it with chapter 12:44. Treasurers had been appointed to keep the chambers before Nehemiah left going back to Persia. When Nehemiah returned to Jerusalem and found that the people were not in Gods' order, he had to re-appoint different treasurers who would be more faithful than the previous ones. There are many individuals who want to be used of God in ministry, but they don't want to be changed nor bear the responsibility or accountability for that particular ministry position. Many are not faithful to what has been assigned to them to do. If you are in a position to appoint someone for a ministry position, you can't appoint them because they are not faithful and won't be faithful! Many have been confronted, but still refuse to listen to sound counsel and instructions. Nehemiah asks God in verse 14, to remember him for the good things he was doing concerning the house of God and the offices associated with it. Perhaps one could think that Nehemiah was being lifted up in pride. I don't believe Nehemiah was "tooting his own horn," but was sincere and humble in his efforts to please the Lord.

In verse 15, Nehemiah once again perceives, (he saw, he noticed, he found out, God showed him) that something else was out of order; that is, Judah was profaning the Sabbath Day. So, he confronts the people regarding their disrespect for the Sabbath. The people were not using the day as a day of rest, a holy day. Trading and selling things, unloading their animals with cargo and merchandise to be sold and bargained for had become the order of the day. The people had no respect for the day that God had hallowed for them as a people of covenant.

When in verse 15, Israel did not respect Gods' Sabbath Day, verse 16 shares with us that others did not respect it as well. Men from Tyre who dwelt in close proximity to Jerusalem, brought fish and other merchandise to sale on the Sabbath day. A lesson here is our actions can cause others to stumble and be in error with the Lord. We may not realize it, but when we disobey God; it not only affects us, but it also has repercussions on those around us. As followers of God, we should always try to set a good example of what God wants out of our lives, so others will have a clear example of the kind of behavior that is expected from a follower of God.

Once again, Nehemiah contended/confronted these orderless people, verse 17, regarding the issue of the Sabbath Day. Nehemiah expected a change in their behavior. The change would restore the order for the Sabbath day. The leader wanted immediate change; not for the people to think about change, nor planning to change but rather a return to what God's word had said for them to do. Until change takes place there is no change, change occurs when you change! In his confrontation, Nehemiah asked the question, "What evil thing is this that ye do, and profane the sabbath day?" This was a rhetorical question from Nehemiah as he already had the answer, but he continued to reason (verse 18) with them for their reason for profaning the sabbath day. Nehemiah reminds the people that in their past behavior, it had evoked the chastisement of God upon them; and now by them profaning the Sabbath day they would bring more of Gods' wrath on them.

As Nehemiah continues to reason with the people, his thinking is based on what Israel had already agreed upon as far as keeping the laws of God. You recall in chapter 10:29-31, the Israelites had put themselves under a "curse" if they would not keep the commandments of God. They promised to do all the commandments and ordinances of the Lord. These commandments included them not giving their daughters and sons over to marry the people of the land. They also promised that they would not buy or trade with merchants on the Sabbath day or on a holy day. Israel had broken both commandments.

As New Testament believers, we don't have a Sabbath Day like Israel did, which we believe to be our Saturdays. We assemble each first day of the week (Sunday) to worship and receive instructions. All our days should be "holy." We ought to live holy all the days of our lives and be in order all week long as well as on the first day of the week. When you live unholy, and rebellious (which is witchcraft) refusing to worship and to give, staying away from church and Christ not focusing on Him; you will get over into "profaning the day."

In verse 19, consider this, for order to take place, order has to be given. Nehemiah said, "I commanded," I give orders; not that I suggested you follow what I said! Nehemiah told the people that when the gates of Jerusalem begin to be dark before the Sabbath; I command that the gates should not be opened till after the Sabbath. He said I also command that there be servants who would serve as watchmen of the gates, that there should no burdens (things that are to be sold) be brought in on the Sabbath day. Some people are uncomfortable with the leader who takes control of the situation under the direction and authority of God. The leader must lead, and the followers should follow.

Verse 20 shows us that merchants and sellers lodged on the outskirts of Jerusalem a few times with their products to be sold. This passage also alerts us to the fact that there will always be some who will test and try the order that has been set. The leader must stand on what he has deemed as coming from the word of God. Many times, people will hang around and perhaps say, "he will weaken and change his stance/stand, then we can go back to what we were doing." By the merchandisers lodging around the wall on the Sabbath, it would be a temptation to lure them on the inside of the walls to continue and profane the Sabbath Day. If the order is from God, then stand even if everyone else wants to walk contrary to that stance.

Nehemiah's strength and authority was expressed on a higher level as we see in verse 21. Nehemiah had to rise up and re-affirm his position as he had to become sterner with his authority because of those who would rebel against the order. A question was asked by Nehemiah, in paraphrasing the question he says, why are those of you still lodging near the wall when you were not supposed to be? These lodgers knew they shouldn't be near the wall but in essence were defying the order that Nehemiah had set, again the order was based on the word of God. I laughed when I read the last portion of this verse. Nehemiah told the rebels that if they continued to dwell by the walls, he would lay hands on them. He is not talking about laying hands on them in prayer! The rebels got the message because they saw that Nehemiah meant what he said to them. The scripture continues by saying that from the time they heard what the leader said, "from that time forth came they no more on the Sabbath!"

Verse 22, Nehemiah gives out another command and this time it was given to the Levites. He tells them that they should cleanse themselves from their participation in profaning the Sabbath or from allowing the people of Judah to profane the Sabbath. He further commands the Levites to keep/guard the gates (keeping evil from coming in there) and to sanctify (make it holy unto the Lord) the Sabbath day. Nehemiah asks God once again (remember, he had said the same thing in verse 14) "remember me, O my God, concerning this also, and spare me according to the greatness of thy mercy." And once again, I don't believe Nehemiah was "tooting his own horn" but was sincere and humble in his efforts to please the Lord. Nehemiah was reminding God that he was doing what God had told him to do even though his obedience was going against the prevailing practices of the people of God. Nehemiah insists that he was honoring God and giving Him pleasure from his life. The testimony of Nehemiah should be our testimony as well.

In verse 10, Nehemiah said he had perceived or that God had revealed something to him and now he says in verse 23 that he saw some other things that were out of order. Before he left Jerusalem the people had agreed that they would not marry the people of the land. After returning, he saw that the Jews had broken their covenant and had married wives of Ashdod, of Ammon and of Moab. These types of unions were against the expressed will of God. If you recall, in chapter 10:30, the people of God had decreed that they would not allow or give their daughters and sons to the people of the land. They made this decree with an oath that they would be "cursed" if they did so! So much for that oath! The people had broken the oath by allowing intermarrying among themselves with those that God had forbidden them to marry. When husbands and wives are out of order, it will affect the children!

Verse 24 says that the children born to these forbidden unions, spake half in the speech of Ashdod and could not speak in the Jew's language! In the latter part of this scripture when it says the children spoke the language of each people, I believe the writer is suggesting that the children could only speak in the language of the non-Jewish parent. Even though the children were not responsible for their births, I have heard it said that sometimes the parent's judgment is often manifested in the children.

In this chapter concerning verses 11, 17 and now in 25, Nehemiah contended with the people. The contention in verse 11 resulted in Nehemiah putting the people in their places. The contention in verse 17 caused Nehemiah to ask questions that caused the people to think about what they were doing. Now, in verses 25, Nehemiah's contending resulted in him being more aggressive with the people. Notice his actions; he curses them - not "cussing" them! Next, he smote/struck or hit some of them. Ok, after reading this verse maybe he did "cuss" them. (lol). I laughed once again when it said Nehemiah plucked (pulled, cut) off their hair! He then made them swear before God that they would not give their daughters and sons to the people of the land to marry, nor would the parents take wives or husbands from the people of the land. The lesson that had been previously taught had to be re-taught.

In verses 26-27 Nehemiah reminded the people about what happened to Solomon when he had allowed himself to marry strange wives from the nations around him. Even though there was no king like Solomon and who was loved by God; the outlandish women he married caused him to sin. Nehemiah reasons that if the marrying of foreigners caused Solomon to sin, it would cause the Jews of his area who enter into these forbidden marriages (Nehemiah calls the marriages "evil") to sin as well. He wanted the people to see they would be causing evil to come upon themselves by marrying the Ammonites and the Moabites people. Nehemiah insisted that he would not listen to their thoughts about believing that there was nothing wrong with these immorally mixed marriages.

Verse 28 causes me to laugh once again. A son of Joiada, the son of Eliashib the high priest, was a son-n-law to Sanballat the Horonite. Do you remember Sanballat? He was a known enemy to Nehemiah and to the advancement of Israel. Here this Jewish man of the high priest household had become a son-in-law to Sanballat. Nehemiah said he chased the rebel away from him! I believe Nehemiah got a "kick" out of chasing this covenant breaker out of his sight. The priesthood had been defiled as well as the covenant and the Levites as viewed by Nehemiah. God's order for the priesthood was out of order! He asks God to remember what these rebels had done, verse 29.

Verses 30-31, shows how this leader took charge of the situation. He cleansed the rebels from all the strangers. This must have been a monumental task but nevertheless it was accomplished by him. Next, Nehemiah now appointed a new group of individuals and gave instructions to them on how to carry out the work of God. Sometimes, in order for change to take place, you have to appoint new leadership. It was clear by their actions that the previous leadership had "dropped the ball."

Nehemiah had maintained his focus on the things of God and was now causing and encouraging the people to maintain the order that had been previously set for them. This order was based on the word of God given to Moses. The layman, the leader and the lover of God, asks God to remember him for the good he had done for the cause of the Lord. I truly believe that God did remember this wonderful man of God, Nehemiah, for focusing and maintaining focus on the assignment God had for his life.

www.ingramcontent.com/pod-product-compliance
Lightning Source LLC
Chambersburg PA
CBHW051530120626
46551CB00012B/1165